Nadiya's Kitchen

Over 100 simple and delicious family recipes

Photography by Holly Pickering

MICHAEL JOSEPH
an imprint of
Penguin Books

Nadiya's Kitchen

Nadiya Hussain

PENGUIN BOOKS

UK | USA | Canada | Ireland | Australia
India | New Zealand | South Africa

Penguin Ireland is part of the Penguin Random House group of companies
whose addresses can be found at global.penguinrandomhouse.com.

First published 2016

006

Text copyright © Nadiya Hussain, 2016
Photography copyright © Holly Pickering, 2016

The moral right of the copyright holders has been asserted

Colour reproduction by Rhapsody Ltd, London
Printed in China by C&C Offset Printing Co., Ltd

A CIP catalogue record for this book is available from the British Library

ISBN : 978-0-718-18451-3

www.greenpenguin.co.uk

MIX
Paper from
responsible sources
FSC® C018179

Penguin Random House is committed to a
sustainable future for our business, our readers
and our planet. This book is made from Forest
Stewardship Council® certified paper.

Contents

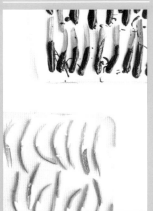

Introduction

It's the room where I sit at the table with a hot cup of tea, as I examine the surface of my worktops for the bit that I missed and challenge myself to see how long it takes before I have to get up and wipe it dry. I never last long enough to have one sip of my tea.

It's the functioning work station where I teeter in front of the kitchen sink, Marigolds on, wrist-deep in foam as I deliberate about the unusual questions I have bouncing around in my head, like why are orangutans orange? And what would grass actually taste like if I cooked it?

It's the ascent where I hop onto a stool, to fight my way onto a worktop for my daily expedition for those shelves that are always overstocked and never in my reach, only for my husband to walk in, get what I need, hand it down and look at me in amusement as I break into a sparkly sweat. Always reconfirming how short I really am.

It's the hub where my children run to straight after school and lift every lid on every pan as they scramble to catch the scent of what I have cooked for tea. Always followed by a rub of a tummy and a large groan of excitement as they leave behind a trail of lunchboxes, jumpers, used tissues and rogue socks in their wake.

It's the shapeshifter that goes from a bright, messy-topped hub of activity, with children, laughter, squabbles and leftovers, to a dim candlelit place of calm and simplicity with a table for two.

It's the only dance floor that gives me enough confidence to grace it with my shapely dance moves, intervened by the odd stir of a pot, checking of a timer or the flick of a switch. The place where I think nobody is watching and someone always is.

It's the factory where I can use every single socket, plug in every piece of equipment I own, make an orchestra of clatter and still it's never, ever too loud.

It's the confession booth that my mum and sister retire to, so we can act like we were cooking around the stove. The place where we risk being caught talking about something naughty, only to quickly reconvene to our appropriate positions at the sound of an approaching voice.

It's the lab where my husband measures every ingredient down to the pinch of salt. The place where each step is crucial and could potentially save him from my judgemental jeering. The place where he proves himself to be more than just the dad who can barbecue.

My kitchen is so much more than a room. It's the place where so much more happens than just cooking or baking. It's the place where I cook for sustenance, bake for love, congregate for company, dance for fun. The exclusive venue for date night, teatime and after-school tantrums. The place where we cook together and everyone's the boss. My kitchen is so much more than my kitchen. It's our kitchen.

This book is a combination of recipes that best reflect the way I cook and bake for my family, focussing on different times of day. Being a mother of three I am candid about the fact that putting things together is also cooking, reflected best in chapters like Midnight Feasts and Lazy Sunday Morning. Dinner Date is all about what I love to eat and cook for when the kids are tucked up in bed. There is something in here for anyone looking for something to make, depending on what you feel like eating and how hard you feel like working for it. It's been a joy writing this book and I hope you can take as much pleasure in reading it and making the recipes from it as I did putting it together.

Lazy Sunday morning

We very rarely get a lazy Sunday morning these days but when we do, it is all the more special. There is nothing better than waking up before the children and creeping down the stairs like a thief in my own home. Trying my hardest to avoid the creaky fifth stair, I discover that the sixth stair is now creaky too (noted for future Sundays). I reach the bottom, only to hear someone stir and greet me with bleary eyes from the top of the stairs, beneath a monumental head of bed hair. The morning cuddles that follow are the warmest of their kind. I flick the kettle on, and the heating (much to the other half's disdain), and tiptoe quickly across the cold floor to have another little snooze on the couch, with the tired sugar lump from the top of the stairs. As the kettle boils and cools I can hear medium-sized feet above making their way from room to room, looking for mum. Finally they all make it down, one by one, for a mum-and-honeys sandwich on the couch. As the sun comes up behind the shutters of our television room we share a few hours of broken sleep, interrupted only by abrupt volume changes and the question of who has taken too much of the fleece, until I realise it may be time to get up properly and feed the brood. The kettle might have boiled twice, maybe even thrice, and it is finally the hour to make something perfect for breakfast – or in our case, borderline brunch. Something to awaken those tired eyes and enthuse the hungry. They say that breakfast is the most important meal of the day . . . though in our house every meal is important.

Scotch pancakes with a mixed berry and lemon thyme compote

Makes about 12

Pancakes and crêpes are favourites in our family. I only have to whisper the word 'pancakes' and I will be bound by some unspoken child's law to produce them. If I cannot make good on the promise immediately, I will be bulldozed for days until they get their pancake fix. On a few occasions I have been known to say 'pancakes' late at night to bribe them to sleep, only to realise that I don't have the time or ingredients to follow through. I have then found myself in the car, in my pyjamas, doing a very much unplanned late-night shop. Nothing beats those faces, though, when they get their pancakes. This is a quick and easy recipe that can made the night before, and can easily be turned into a crêpe recipe if you add extra milk to loosen the batter. Paired with mixed berry and lemon thyme compote, the combination is sublime. Sometimes I wonder why my children are so unwavering in their quest for pancakes . . . but I only have to eat one to understand.

For the compote

400g mixed frozen berries

100g caster sugar

3 sprigs of lemon thyme, leaves picked

1 tablespoon lemon juice

For the pancakes

225g plain flour

½ teaspoon cream of tartar

½ teaspoon bicarbonate of soda

1 tablespoon caster sugar

½ teaspoon fine sea salt

1 large egg, beaten

200ml whole milk

25g unsalted butter, for frying

For the sweetened yoghurt

300ml natural Greek yoghurt

4 tablespoons runny honey

Prep: 15 minutes   **Cook:** 30 minutes

❄: **Pancakes can be frozen after frying**

To make the compote: Put the frozen mixed berries in a medium saucepan along with the caster sugar, lemon thyme leaves and lemon juice.

Cook over a gentle heat for 15 minutes, until the fruit is soft and macerated.

Take off the heat and set the compote aside while you make the pancakes.

To make the pancakes: Sift the flour, cream of tartar and bicarbonate of soda into a bowl. Stir in the caster sugar and salt.

Make a well in the centre, and add the egg and milk. Give everything a good mix until you get a really nice thick batter. At this point you can just put it in the fridge to use the next day.

Heat a non-stick frying pan over a low to medium heat. Drop a small knob of butter into the pan, and leave it to melt.

Drop 3–4 tablespoons of the pancake mixture into the pan, leaving space between each for the pancakes to spread as they cook, and leave for 2–3 minutes until bubbles cover the surface of the pancakes.

Now, using a rounded palette knife turn over and brown the other side for another 2–3 minutes. Lift on to a warmed plate. Wipe any burnt bits out of the pan with kitchen paper, and add a fresh knob of butter.

Use up all the batter in this way, keeping the cooked pancakes on a plate covered in foil.

To make the sweetened yoghurt: Mix the yoghurt and the honey together. To serve, take a few warm pancakes, and add a large dollop of sweetened yoghurt and a generous serving of compote.

Blueberry caraway scones

Makes 7–8

These scones are such an easy way to get anyone, even the kids, involved in the kitchen – the steps to making them are so simple. Dried blueberries are a welcome change from the more standard sultanas, but you can use any dried fruit you have at home. I have also added caraway seeds, which remind me of that medicine Mum would give us for tummy aches. Yeah, you all know which one I'm talking about! The one you would secretly sneak a swig of if you happened to be passing the cupboard . . . or maybe even fake a tummy ache in the hope that she would give you teaspoon before bed. I'm no saint: I would lie through my teeth for some gripe water. I'm not saying these will taste of gripe water, you understand, but occasionally biting into one of the seeds in the scone gives a similar explosion of flavour. Buttered generously and eaten warm, these are delightful with a cup of hot tea.

225g self-raising flour, plus extra for rolling

a pinch of salt

55g unsalted butter

25g caster sugar

100g dried blueberries

1 tablespoon caraway seeds, ground with a pestle and mortar

150ml milk

1 medium egg, beaten

Prep: 15 minutes   Cook: **12 minutes**   ❄: **Can be frozen**

Preheat the oven to 220°C/fan 200°C. Lightly grease a baking sheet.

Mix the flour and salt in a bowl. Rub in the butter with your fingertips until it resembles breadcrumbs. To the bowl add the sugar, dried blueberries and crushed caraway seeds. Mix everything together.

Add the milk, and bring the dough roughly together using a rounded spatula. Then bring the dough together more by hand, and put it on a floured surface. Don't be tempted to overwork or knead the dough, as this will result in a bit of a tough scone.

Roll out the dough to about 2cm thick and use a 5cm cutter to cut out rounds, making sure to make straight cuts down and not to twist (this will stop your scones from leaning). Re-roll any leftover scraps and cut out more scones. Place the scones on the baking sheet, brush the tops with egg, and bake for 12–15 minutes. They should be lightly golden.

Cool on a wire rack, then serve with lashings of butter or clotted cream and jam.

Tip: If you don't have a pestle and mortar, try my grandma's make-shift version – an empty can and the rounded end of a rolling pin.

Breakfast halwa croissants

Makes 12–14

These croissants are a labour of love, and I always pull this recipe out when we have guests over to stay. In my house, guests don't get a decent night's sleep because my kids are up at the crack of dawn, but I do try to make up for it with a decent breakfast. Halwa is a classic Bangladeshi breakfast dish that is served with a kind of flaky-pastry flatbread. So I figured rather than having two separate components, why not have an all-in-one … something that can be eaten sitting down or on the go, which is often the case for my husband. The pastry and filling can be made the night before and assembled first thing. This recipe makes plenty of halwa, and it's great eaten warm as a snack or spread on buttered toast. See the step-by-step photographs on pages 18–19.

For the croissants

500g strong white bread flour

80g caster sugar

10g fine sea salt (plus a pinch for the egg wash)

10g instant yeast

300ml cold water

300g butter, chilled

1 medium egg, beaten with a pinch of fine sea salt

For the halwa

15g each of pistachios and cashews, roasted and chopped

75g coarse semolina

75g caster sugar

75g unsalted butter, melted

150ml boiling water

½ teaspoon each of cardamom and cinnamon powder

25g currants

Prep: **1 hour 20 minutes for the croissants, plus overnight chilling time; 10 minutes for the halwa**   Cook: **20 minutes per croissant batch; 30 minutes for the halwa**   ❅: **Can be frozen after shaping, before the final prove**

First put the flour in a stand mixer bowl, with the sugar and salt on one side and the yeast on the other. Add the cold water, and mix on slow with a dough hook for 2 minutes, then on medium for 6 minutes. Tip the dough out on a floured surface, flatten it, then wrap it up and leave it in the fridge for 1 hour.

Again on a floured surface, roll out the chilled dough to a 60 x 20cm rectangle, 1cm thick. Flatten the chilled butter into a 40 x 19cm rectangle by placing it between two sheets of baking parchment and bashing with a rolling pin, then roll to the right size.

Now place the butter on the bottom two-thirds of the dough (the short side of the dough rectangle is nearest you). Fold the exposed top part of the dough over, and the bottom third of the dough with the butter on top over that. There should be two layers of butter, and three of dough. Pinch the edges, wrap in clingfilm and chill for 1 hour.

Take the dough out of the fridge. Imagining the dough is a book, put the dough on the surface with the folded 'spine' on the left and the flap on top of the dough on the right-hand side, and roll out to a 60 x 20cm rectangle. Once again, fold the top third down and the bottom third up. Pinch the edges, and chill. This is the first turn.

Repeat the previous step twice more, giving three turns in total. Leave the dough to chill overnight.

Roll the dough out on a floured surface to a thickness of 7mm (about 35cm x 65 cm). Trim the edges with a dough or pizza cutter. Cut into two rectangles about 16 x 60cm, and then into equilateral triangles with sides about 15cm long. Leave the triangles to chill while you make the halwa.

To make the halwa: Roast the nuts in the oven for 15 minutes at 180°C/fan 160°C.

Put the semolina in a large, deep saucepan and toast for about 10 minutes. Stir regularly with a wooden spoon to make sure the semolina doesn't burn. Don't be disheartened by how long this takes. I promise the toasted semolina makes all the difference. Once it is a strong brown colour, add the sugar and butter. Once everything is well combined, add the boiling water.

The mixture will bubble up. Keep mixing for about 4 minutes, until it all comes together.

Take it off the heat, then add the spices, nuts and currants. Pour it into a bowl and leave it to cool.

To assemble the croissants: Preheat the oven to 200°C/fan 180°C.

Take one of the triangles and stretch the pointy end slightly. Place a heaped teaspoon of halwa on the base of each triangle. Roll up to the tapered end, and put the croissant on a baking sheet, then repeat to make all the croissants. Put the baking tray in a large plastic bag, and leave the croissants for 2 hours to prove.

Brush the proved croissants with the egg wash, and bake in the oven for 15–20 minutes. They should be lightly golden and easily come away from the baking sheet.

Leave to cool on a wire rack.

Skillet crumpets with salted honey butter

Makes about 35

Words cannot express how accomplished I felt when I first made crumpets. I watched the bubbles rise to the surface and thought to myself 'I'm making crumpets!' I tried to resist the urge to call mum, but did it anyway (she was far from impressed at 7am). I know it's easy to buy a packet, and even I do so on busy weekdays, but this recipe can be made in advance, and the batter will keep in the fridge for a few days. They can even be heated through in a low oven and served for brunch the next day.

For the salted honey butter

250g salted butter

4 tablespoons set honey

½ teaspoon fine sea salt

For the crumpets

230g strong white bread flour

230g plain white flour

1 teaspoon cream of tartar

7g fast-action yeast

500ml lukewarm water

1 teaspoon sea salt

½ teaspoon bicarbonate of soda

280ml lukewarm milk

vegetable oil, for frying

Prep: 25 minutes, plus 1 hour 30 minutes resting
Cook: 1 hour, or less if frying in batches   ❄: Can be frozen

To make the salted honey butter: Put the butter into a mixing bowl, and mix to loosen it. Increase the speed and add the honey and salt. Mix for 3 minutes on a medium speed until everything is well incorporated. Put the honey butter in a bowl, cover and leave in the fridge to chill. It can be kept in the fridge for a week, or frozen for two months when wrapped up as a log in clingfilm.

To make the crumpets: Sift both the flours, the cream of tartar and the yeast into a bowl. Then stir in the lukewarm water using a wooden spoon, and cover with clingfilm. Leave for 1 hour; the dough will rise and then fall back down again.

Uncover the bowl and sprinkle in the sea salt, mix again with a wooden spoon, cover and leave for another 30 minutes.

Stir the bicarbonate of soda into the lukewarm milk, then stir this into the batter with a wooden spoon. It should be a thick, pourable consistency.

Heat a flat non-stick frying pan until it is very hot. Use two pans if you have them, so you can fry the crumpets in batches. Using a piece of kitchen paper, grease the pan lightly with oil, then ladle in the batter to make crumpets that are about 8cm across. Cook for 3 minutes on one side – the underside should be brown and the top should have small holes all over it. Flip, and cook for a further 3 minutes.

Put the cooked crumpets in a low oven (120°C/fan 100°C) to keep warm while you fry the rest.

Smother with the salted honey butter to serve.

Kipper kedgeree

Serves 6–8

Now, I know kippers have a bit of a reputation for being smelly and perhaps not very fashionable, so naturally the thought of cooking with kipper left me a little bit wary. However, kedgeree is something that we eat often in my culture. Rice is also grown in abundance in Bangladesh, and used in every meal of the day, including breakfast. This tradition hasn't changed too much among those who moved here decades ago. As a lover of all fish, even I can be taken aback by the strong smell of kippers, but it's worth it: the flavour is out of this world. It has an intense smokiness. The flesh is tender and a beautiful golden hue, with a subtle saltiness. Once it blends with the lovely flavours and textures of the kedgeree you have a marriage made in heaven. I can happily announce I am no longer afraid of kippers, and neither should you be.

250g basmati rice

2 teaspoons cumin seeds

2 teaspoons coriander seeds

5 tablespoons olive oil

2 teaspoons salt

2 large onions, peeled and sliced

½ teaspoon cayenne pepper

½ teaspoon garam masala

6 large eggs

225g frozen peas

500g cooked, smoked kipper or mackerel fillets, flaked

50ml double cream

2 tablespoons chopped coriander (about 1 small pack)

2 tablespoons chopped chives (about ½ small pack)

Prep: 25 minutes   **Cook: 35 minutes**   ❄: **Cannot be frozen**

Put the rice in a large saucepan, and add 750ml cold water. Place on the hob and bring to the boil, before reducing to a simmer and cooking for 10–12 minutes, until the rice still has a little bite to it. Drain in a colander, rinse with cold water and set aside.

Crush the cumin and coriander seeds in a pestle and mortar. Warm the oil in a large frying pan, then add the salt and the crushed spices. Lightly toast over a low heat for 1–2 minutes.

Now add the sliced onions, and cook gently. Add the cayenne pepper and garam masala. Put the lid on and cook for 10 minutes over a very low heat.

While the onions are cooking, put the eggs in a pan of cold water, bring to the boil then reduce to a simmer and cook for 6 minutes. They should have a slightly soft centre. Drain, peel and put the eggs in a bowl of cold water. Cut them into quarters just before placing them on top of the kedgeree.

Add the frozen peas to the onion mix, and stir through, then add the flaked kippers. Add the cooked rice and mix through, making sure to incorporate everything really well. Finally add the cream to loosen the mixture and add an extra bit of luxury to the dish.

Serve on a large platter, with the quartered eggs arranged on top, and sprinkled with the chives and coriander.

Chocolate and hazelnut brioche loaf

Serves 8

It's so tempting to pick up a packet of individually wrapped brioche for the kids as they squirm in the trolley. (Squirming purely to be annoying, because you're trying to do the entire weekly shop in a window of about 20 minutes; squirming because they want to be released and go wild in the aisles.) I won't lie: I bought that packet of brioche . . . and why not – it's quick and easy, and kids love it. But I really wanted to try my hand at a homemade version. This a great enriched bread dough to start working with, especially as you can prove it overnight in the fridge. You don't have to watch it like some doughs, or worry about why it hasn't risen after an hour. I like to add chocolate to the dough – not because the kids love it, but because I love it – and this is quite delicious straight out of the oven. Just remember to take a slice along with you on those dreaded weekly shops, to keep hunger at bay.

380g strong white bread flour, plus extra for dusting

7g fine sea salt

7g fast-action yeast

4 medium eggs

4 tablespoons milk, approx.

175g unsalted butter, cut into small pieces, plus extra for greasing

100g dark chocolate chips

100g hazelnuts, roasted and chopped

I egg, beaten with a pinch of sea salt,

Prep: 40 minutes, plus at least 4½ hours for resting and proving
Cook: 45 minutes to 1 hour   ❊: **Can be frozen**

Put the flour in a mixing bowl. Add the salt on one side and the yeast on the other.

Break the four eggs into a measuring jug and beat with a fork, then add enough milk to make up 250ml of liquid. Now add the liquid to the dry ingredients already in the bowl.

Mix either by hand or in a stand mixer (with a dough hook attached). The dough should come together, leaving no flour at the bottom of the bowl. If there is flour left, add a little more liquid just to bring it together.

On a lightly floured surface work the dough by hand for 10 minutes until it is firmer and more elastic, or use the mixer at a low speed for 6 minutes. Now slowly add little knobs of butter until they are incorporated; the butter should be smoothly streaked throughout the mixture. This takes about 6–8 minutes.

Scrape the dough out of the bowl, put it in a clean bowl and cover tightly with clingfilm. Place in the fridge for at least 2 hours, or you can do this just before bed and leave it to prove overnight.

Take the dough out of the fridge and knock it back to deflate it. Form it into a ball, place back in the bowl, cover with clingfilm again and put it back in the fridge for another hour.

Preheat the oven to 200°C/fan 180°C.

Grease a loaf tin with butter and line it with a strip of greaseproof paper, with enough overhang at the ends to help you pull out the brioche after baking.

On a lightly floured surface knead the dough for 1 minute, then add the chocolate chips and hazelnuts, kneading until they are evenly distributed. Now form the dough into a loaf shape, making sure to pinch the bottom seam. Put the brioche into the tin, then put the tin in a large plastic bag and leave to prove for 1½ hours.

Glaze the top of the loaf with the beaten egg. Bake for 15 minutes, then reduce the temperature to 160°C/fan 140°C and bake for a further 30 minutes. When you take the brioche out it should sound hollow when you tap the bottom. If it doesn't, put it back into the oven for 5 minutes more, checking until you get that hollow sound.

Leave to cool on a wire rack.

Feta and dill savoury muffins

Makes 12

I know when you hear the word 'muffin' you probably think of the blueberry or chocolate chip variety. However, muffins can be so much more. According to my husband, muffins are meant to be sweet, but I tend to veer in the direction of a savoury muffin accompanied by a sweet cup of tea – perhaps mainly to prove to him that I am always right. He took some convincing, because he's not a feta cheese fan, but these are so good: the cooked feta melts down slightly in the muffin, keeping its distinctive salty flavour. The dill adds such a fresh taste, and the crunch of the seeds gives an extra dimension to the texture. These can be eaten fresh out of the oven or cooled, sliced, smothered in cream cheese and topped with smoked salmon. And now when I say muffin, my husband answers, 'Dill and feta, please!'

175g plain flour

50g wholewheat flour

2½ teaspoons baking powder

1 teaspoon fine salt

275ml whole milk

1 medium egg

100g cottage cheese

75g unsalted butter, melted and cooled

50g feta cheese, crumbled

½ teaspoon wholegrain mustard

2 tablespoons fresh dill, chopped

1 teaspoon ground black pepper

8 sundried tomatoes, chopped

25g pumpkin seeds

Prep: 15 minutes   Cook: 20–25 minutes   ❄: Can be frozen

Preheat the oven to 200°C/fan 180°C. Line a 12-hole muffin tin with cases.

Put the flours, baking powder and salt in a bowl, and stir everything together.

Now add the milk, egg, cottage cheese, melted butter, feta cheese, mustard, dill and black pepper. Mix it all together and spoon into muffin cases.

Top each muffin with a little chopped sundried tomato and sprinkle with the pumpkin seeds.

Bake in the oven for 20–25 minutes, or until a skewer inserted comes out clean.

Maple porridge with warm pineapple and lime

Serves 2

I'm all too happy to admit, like many I'm sure, that I am not a massive porridge fan. It reminds me of when my dad was poorly in hospital and discovered it. On his return home he decided to lay down a new law in the Jamir household: 'Porridge every day, forever.' I struggled for years afterwards to even bring myself to look at the stuff. It was only when I had my own kids that I realised how good it actually was as a slow-release breakfast, for children and grown-ups alike. So I tinkered away with normal porridge – only to confirm, ten years on, that I still didn't like it in its natural state. However, I did find a divine combination, in which maple syrup adds an earthy sweetness, and sweet crunchy pineapple with the zing of lime uplifts the whole thing. Dad says my porridge is too posh for him, so I still make him his hospital porridge now and again. But little by little he asks less often for his version, rather, 'I'll have your posh porridge if you're making any.'

For the porridge

100g rolled porridge oats

a pinch of salt

500ml whole milk

1–2 tablespoons maple syrup, or more to taste

For the pineapple and lime

400g fresh or tinned pineapple chunks

20g caster sugar

zest of 1 lime

juice of ½ lime

Prep: **10 minutes**　Cook: **15 minutes**　❄: **Cannot be frozen**

To make the porridge: Put the oats in a medium saucepan with the salt, and pour over the milk.

Cook over a low to medium heat, stirring regularly, for about 10 minutes or until the oats are tender to the touch and the porridge is thick and creamy (if you want a thinner consistency, add more milk).

Take the porridge off the heat and stir the maple syrup through.

To make the pineapple and lime: In a medium saucepan, while the porridge is cooking, place the pineapple, sugar, lime zest and juice and cook over a low to medium heat for 7 minutes, or until the pineapple has softened, thickened and gently caramelised.

To serve: Top the porridge with the fruit mixture while everything is still warm.

Nutmeg baked eggs with watercress

Serves 4

My dad is a massive egg fiend, and I always try out egg recipes on him. He raises chickens and ducks in his back garden, so he always has a fresh supply for me when I visit. He will try any new dish, but especially if it has eggs in it. Many years ago I really wanted to impress him with my baked eggs, and I came up with this simple and reliable dish, baked in individual ramekins, which satisfies the greediest of eaters – especially me. Breaking through the egg to reveal the runny yolk, with the deliciously wilted watercress and a hint of nutmeg, makes for a worthwhile breakfast. It's also a great recipe for adapting to suit your taste. My dad would add a dash of Tabasco to the egg once it's out of the oven, but then he adds a little heat to everything. The kids add ketchup. I add cheese. It's yours to play with as you will.

450g fresh watercress

25g salted butter, plus extra for greasing

½ teaspoon freshly grated nutmeg

4 large eggs

4 tablespoons double cream

4 tablespoons mature Cheddar cheese, finely grated

salt and freshly ground black pepper

Prep: 10 minutes   Cook: **15 minutes**   ❄: **Cannot be frozen**

Preheat the oven to 190°C/fan 170°C. Butter 4 dishes (approximately 12cm in diameter) and set them aside. Bring a large sauce pan of water to the boil, then take it off the heat.

Push all the watercress into the just-boiled water. Leave for 3 minutes, which will allow the watercress to wilt slightly. Drain it in a colander, and squeeze out any excess water by twisting in a clean tea towel. Chop the drained watercress roughly then place in a bowl and to this add half of the butter, and the nutmeg, and season with salt and pepper.

Divide the watercress between the ramekins, and break an egg into each. Season again with salt and pepper.

Pour a tablespoon of cream into each ramekin, and sprinkle over the grated cheese. Add a knob of butter to each ramekin.

Bake for 10–12 minutes, until the eggs are just set.

Caper, mustard and chive soldiers with soft-boiled eggs

Serves 2

So who doesn't love boiled eggs and soldiers? I do and so do my kids, and some might say we are a little over-enthusiastic. As a parent, and as a daughter of very good cooks, I am always looking for new flavour combinations. We were taught as children, especially by my dad, to try everything . . . if it was edible, we should give it a go. So now I love adding an unexpected twist to something ordinary. I'm not saying that ordinary soldiers and eggs are not a thing of beauty, but here the saltiness of the capers on the toast, with the kick of mustard and the freshness of chives works really well with unseasoned runny yolk. These quantities make plenty of butter – it's great to use when baking fish, or for rubbing under the skin of a chicken before roasting. Wrapped in clingfilm, it will keep in the freezer for two months.

2 tablespoons capers, drained

2 teaspoons English mustard

2 tablespoons chopped chives

180g salted butter

4 large eggs

4 slices of toast

Prep: **10 minutes**   Cook: **6 minutes**

Put the capers, mustard, chives and butter in a food processor. Whizz the mixture for about 3 seconds, until everything is incorporated. Put the butter on a piece of clingfilm and roll it into a cigar shape before popping it in the fridge. This way, you can slice pieces off as you need them once the butter is frozen.

Boil an egg to your preferred consistency. I like a soft-boiled egg, as the runny yolk works so well with the soldiers. To do this, put fridge-cold eggs into a small pan of cold water. Bring it to the boil, then turn down the heat and simmer for 4 minutes.

Spread the toast generously with the butter mixture, and slice into soldiers.

One-wok red onion and bread stir-fry

Serves 2

This has to be one of the most nostalgic breakfast recipes – it takes me right back. This was my mum's thrifty way of using up bread that was very close to its sell-by date, with ingredients she always had at home, like onions, chillies and coriander. Bread never lasts long enough in our house to go out of date, but I make this recipe just for the trip down memory lane. When you toast the bread in the pan long enough for it to get crispy, the onions soften and the cooked-out chillies will mellow. Finally add the egg to weld it all together, with a dash of fresh coriander. It makes for the heartiest breakfast, and we still eat it the way I did twenty years ago – all together in a circle on the floor, with six forks.

3 tablespoons sunflower oil

1 tablespoon salted butter

1 medium red onion, sliced

1 small chilli deseeded and chopped finely (you can leave it out if you don't want to add it)

½ teaspoon fine sea salt

1 teaspoon ground black pepper

5 slices of bread, cut into 2cm cubes

3 large eggs, whisked lightly

3 tablespoons chopped coriander (1 small pack)

Prep: 15 minutes   **Cook: 15 minutes**   ❄: **Cannot be frozen**

Heat a wok over a medium heat. Put the oil and butter into the hot wok.

Add the onions and chilli, lower the heat and cook gently for about 10 minutes, until softened. Season with salt and pepper.

Now add the cubes of bread, and toss through the onions to mix well. The bread will become lightly toasted.

Pour the eggs all over the bread. Give everything a brief stir, then cover with a lid and leave over a low heat for 2 minutes. This will allow the egg to cook through.

Take off the lid and stir the mixture to break it up.

Take off the heat, sprinkle over the coriander and serve.

Tip: This recipe tastes even nicer the following day so save up that stale bread and double the quantities to make plenty of leftovers.

Sharing lunch

On a day when we are all home together, gathering the troops for lunch can be a battle of wills. We are all scattered about the house doing our own thing: husband on call, tinkering away on his laptop; the children in their rooms with doors left wide open to know that I'm around. It's a comfort thing, I feel safe when I can hear them, and they feel safe when they can hear me. One is reading David Walliams's latest and laughing quietly into the pages. Another is building the Eiffel Tower out of Lego, grunting sporadically when he can't get a stubborn brick to detach itself. The last is relentlessly pressing the tummy of her favourite doll so she can sing along with her every time, perfecting her singing voice (a work-in-progress). It's no mean feat trying to get them all together in one place. My secret weapon? I only have to shout from the bottom of the stairs, 'Shall we make lunch together?' That's enough to cause a stampede of three scrambling down the curved stairs, all shouting out their ideas of what they would like to eat (and no, ice cream does not make a lunch!) Suddenly it really is like a military operation: it's all hands on deck, everyone has their orders and there's strictly no squabbling!

Shallot-dressed crispy grilled salmon salad

Serves 5 as a main

For the shallot dressing

150ml rice vinegar

150ml water

85g palm sugar

1.5cm piece of root ginger, peeled and crushed to a paste with a pestle and mortar

1 clove of garlic, crushed

a pinch of salt

225g shallots, peeled and finely diced

½ teaspoon chilli flakes

For the salmon salad

3 courgettes, cut into ribbons with a peeler

3 tablespoons olive oil, for frying

salt and freshly ground black pepper, to taste

5 x 180g salmon fillets

12 cherry tomatoes, halved

1 medium carrot, cut into ribbons with a peeler

½ red pepper, thinly sliced

1 yellow pepper, thinly sliced

3 handfuls of rocket leaves

1 large handful of coriander leaves (½ small pack)

Being raised in a Bangladeshi household, fish was an absolute staple: cured, dried, fermented and fresh. But for some reason my mum never ventured out of her comfort zone, and always preferred fish that came from Indian waters. She said it had a different smell – the smell of home. She is great cook, and also has a nose for sourcing this kind of fish from specialist shops. But as a busy mother with young kids I always go for the supermarket fish that I can throw in the same basket as my cereal, eggs and toothpaste! Salmon is therefore a firm favourite in our home. Here the crispy skin of the salmon paired with the cool, flavoursome salad makes an amazing lunch.

Prep: 25 minutes   Cook: 25 minutes   ❄: Cannot be frozen

To make the shallot dressing: Put the vinegar, water, palm sugar, ginger and garlic in a pan and boil until the sugar has dissolved. Strain to get rid of the garlic and ginger. Set the liquid aside, and leave it to cool.

Put the shallots and chilli flakes into a bowl, and pour over the cooled vinegar mixture. The dressing can be stored in the fridge until you need it.

To make the salmon salad: Heat the griddle until very hot. Mix the ribboned courgettes with a tablespoon of olive oil, and put them on the griddle. Cook for a minute on each side. Transfer to a bowl, season with salt and set aside.

Rub the salmon all over with another two tablespoons of olive oil. Place on the hot griddle, skin side down. Don't move it, or the skin will tear. Be patient, and it will slowly become opaque and cook right through. After 15 minutes, place the griddle pan in the oven at 200°C/fan 180°C for 7 minutes to finish cooking. Remove from the oven and season generously.

Put the tomatoes, carrot, red and yellow pepper in a bowl, add 2 tablespoons of the dressing and give everything a good mix. Now add the rocket leaves, coriander, another 2 tablespoons of the dressing and mix again.

Tip the salad out on to a platter and place the pieces of fish on top. Drizzle generously with some more dressing.

Sticky chicken with apple and bean salad

Serves 4

For the chicken

4 chicken drumsticks, skin on and bone in

4 chicken thighs, skin on and bone in

1 teaspoon cumin seeds

1 teaspoon fennel seeds

1 teaspoon cinnamon

½ teaspoon smoked paprika

1 tablespoon sunflower oil

1 tablespoon tomato purée

1 tablespoon vinegar

2 tablespoons dark muscovado sugar

2 tablespoons apple juice

For the salad

juice and zest of 1 lime

1 large green apple (skin on), cored and diced the same size as the black-eyed peas

400g can black-eyed peas, drained

a large handful of coriander, chopped

1 red onion, diced the same size as the black-eyed peas

1 red pepper, diced the same size as the black-eyed peas

Mealtimes can be messy with greedy little hands in full swing, but this is particularly true when this sticky chicken's on the table. Using thighs and drumsticks rather than breasts keeps the chicken nice and moist, and its sweet, spicy flavour works really well with the soft beans and the tart, crunchy apple salad. Kitchen roll is a must – you've been warned!

Prep: **20 minutes**   Cook: **40 minutes**   ❄: **Chicken can be frozen after marinating**

To make the chicken: Preheat the oven to 180°C/fan 160°C.

Slash each of the chicken pieces three or four times; this will allow the flavours to get right down to the bone. Put the chicken pieces in a roasting tin.

In a small bowl, mix together the cumin seeds, fennel seeds, cinnamon, smoked paprika, sunflower oil, tomato purée, vinegar, muscovado sugar and apple juice. Pour over the chicken and give everything a good mix by hand, and work the spices into the slashes in the chicken.

Bake the chicken for 40 minutes. Turn the pieces after the first 20 minutes, and spoon over the pan juices. Check the chicken is cooked by piercing it close to the bone; if the juices run clear it is done. Place on a plate and cover with foil while you prepare the salad.

In the meantime, prepare the salad.

To make the salad: Put the lime juice and zest in a bowl. Add the chopped apple to the lime juice and zest, and give it a good stir, then set aside. This will stop the apple browning while you prepare the other things.

Add the coriander, red onion, beans and red pepper to the salad. Give everything a good mix before serving alongside the chicken.

Chicken pasta with kale and pistachio pesto

Serves 4

Pesto is a go-to ingredient when I want to make a quick lunch. I only discovered that I could make my own pesto using foraged wild garlic a few years ago (that's a whole other recipe)… I used to buy it in jars until I realised how easy it is to make and store, and started experimenting. This unusual blend of kale and pistachios makes a vibrant green pesto, with the pistachios adding a very subtle sweetness. Mixed with the chicken and the pasta, it makes such a heartwarming dish that isn't at all time-consuming to prepare. In fact it is really satisfying to see such a quick dish come together, and yet know that you didn't have to dial any numbers to get it.

350g pasta (fusilli or penne work well)

For the pesto

100g kale, stalks removed

3 cloves of garlic

50g pistachios, toasted

4 tablespoons olive oil

salt and freshly ground black pepper, to taste

For the chicken

2 tablespoons olive oil

3 large chicken breasts, cut into chunks

a small handful of basil, finely chopped

zest of 1 lemon

salt and freshly ground black pepper, to taste

Prep: **20 minutes**   Cook: **15 minutes**   ❄: **Cannot be frozen**

Bring a large pan of salted water to the boil, and cook the pasta following the instructions on the packet.

While the pasta is cooking, put a large frying pan over a medium heat and add the oil. Add the chicken and the basil, and cook for 8–10 minutes, or until the chicken is cooked through.

While the chicken is cooking you can get started on the pesto. Put all the ingredients into a food processor with 1 tablespoon of water, and whizz until you have a paste. Season with salt and pepper to taste.

Drain the cooked pasta (reserving the cooking water), mix through the chicken and then add all of the pesto. Sprinkle over the lemon zest, and give everything a thorough mix before serving. If the mix is a bit dry, add a splash (about 100ml) of the reserved cooking water.

Chilli cheese burritos

Serves 4 (2 wraps each)

I love making chilli and I am a massive fan of one-pot cooking. Not only because it's easier, but because a one-pot meal can give you scope for so many other dishes. This chilli is a quick and easy recipe that can be cooked on the stove, or in the slow cooker ready for when you get home from work. This is one of those meals where you can sit down with bowls full of ingredients and customise according to your taste and appetite. The warm tortilla wrapped around the rice, chilli and cheese is a winning combo. I like to add an extra bowl of raw onions and jalapeños for the more adventurous members of our family. This recipe makes plenty, as leftovers are great to use in jacket potatoes or pasta.

For the chilli

1 tablespoon olive oil

1 medium onion, peeled and finely chopped

3 garlic cloves, peeled and crushed

500g lean lamb or beef mince

700g passata

400g red kidney beans, drained and rinsed

1 tablespoon ground cumin

1 teaspoon mild chilli powder

salt and freshly ground black pepper

To serve

8 corn tortillas

200g cooked white rice (about 85g uncooked)

125g Cheddar cheese, grated

125g soured cream

large handful of coriander, roughly chopped (½ small packet)

Prep: 15 minutes   Cook: 30 minutes   ❄: Chilli can be frozen

Heat the oil in a large frying pan, then add the garlic and onion. Cook for 10 minutes over a low to medium heat until the onion has softened. Remove from the pan and place in a bowl.

Add the mince to the same pan and cook for another 5 minutes, until brown, using a wooden spoon to separate out the strands. Add the onions back into the pan.

Now add the passata, kidney beans, cumin, chilli powder and salt and pepper to taste. Stir and cook over a medium heat for 15 minutes, until thickened.

Meanwhile, have all the other elements ready on the table so everyone can make their own burrito. Warm the tortillas in the oven for 5 minutes at 220°C/fan 200°C, or use the instructions on the back of the packet.

Deep pan black olive and tuna pizza

Serves 6

I travelled to Italy not long ago with my baby brother, Shak, and husband as a treat to my brother for doing so well in his exams. We went as pizza novices, and came back with a very different appreciation of the dish. All you have to do is dial a number, and you can have a pizza delivered fresh to your door. But a homemade one beats a takeaway hands down, every single time. It's worth the all the time and the effort. What's more, it's a great way to cook together, and it's even better to eat together. Once you have the dough recipe sorted, the toppings are yours to play with. This pizza is a very simple store-cupboard staple with its tomato base, salty olives and tuna.

For the base

500g strong white bread flour, plus extra for dusting

7g fast-action yeast

2 teaspoons fine sea salt

3 tablespoons olive oil, plus extra for brushing and greasing

300ml lukewarm water

For the topping

250g passata

7 anchovy fillets

½ red onion, peeled and sliced

100g pitted black olives, sliced

1 can of tuna flakes in oil, drained

3 garlic cloves, thinly sliced

freshly ground black pepper, to taste

Prep: **30 minutes, plus resting**   Cook: **50 minutes**

❄: **Can be frozen, once topped**

To make the base: Put the flour in a bowl, and add the yeast to one side and the salt to the other.

Make a well in the centre and add the 3 tablespoons of oil, then gradually add the water and stir everything together with a rounded spatula. Using your hands, bring the dough together, then put it on a floured surface and knead for 10 minutes, until smooth and elastic.

Shape the dough into a ball and put it in a lightly oiled bowl. Cover it with clingfilm and leave it to rise for 1 hour, or until it has doubled in size.

Preheat the oven to 220°C/fan 200°C.

Remove the dough from the bowl and put it on a lightly oiled baking tray. Use your fingertips to gently push it into a rectangle, about 30 x 24cm. Brush the top lightly with olive oil, cover with clingfilm and leave it to rise for another 40 minutes. Take the clingfilm off and make indentations all over the dough with your fingertips, and flatten it. This will allow for large pockets of flavour on top of the pizza.

Top the pizza base with the passata, followed by the onion, black olives, tuna and sliced garlic, then top with the anchovies. Leave a 1cm border all the way around the pizza. Sprinkle with black pepper

If properly flattened, the pizza should only need 30 minutes baked in an oven at 220°C/fan 200°C, although it may take longer.

Griddled halloumi with a pomegranate salsa

Serves 6 as a light lunch

I have a senseless love affair with cheese, but I only discovered halloumi when I went to a branch of Nando's and couldn't eat the chicken there. Forced into a corner, I had no choice but to order the vegetarian option. Deep down I wanted chicken, and I wanted it now, and all I wanted to do was run out of the restaurant and satisfy my need for grilled chicken . . . But I'm the kind of person who is too scared to exchange a top that doesn't fit, for fear of upsetting the cashier. So halloumi it was! And it was good halloumi – I was so annoyed with myself for not trying this delicious cheese sooner. I even bought a few chunks of it on my way home. The griddled halloumi softens, but doesn't melt enough to become gooey, and mixed with the pomegranate salad it makes for an amazingly light (yet cheesy) lunch.

½ red onion, roughly chopped

150g cherry tomatoes, roughly chopped

2 tablespoons roughly chopped flat-leaf parsley (⅔ small pack)

2 tablespoons chopped fresh mint leaves (⅔ small pack)

4 tablespoons olive oil

2 tablespoons pomegranate molasses

½ teaspoon chilli flakes

500g halloumi, cut into ½cm slices

seeds from half a pomegranate

salt, to taste

Prep: 15 minutes   Cook: **10 minutes**   ❄: Cannot be frozen

Put the chopped red onion and cherry tomatoes in a mixing bowl.

Add the herbs, 2 tablespoons of the olive oil, the pomegranate molasses, the chilli flakes and a generous pinch of salt, and mix everything together. Set the salsa aside.

Heat 2 tablespoons oil in a non-stick frying pan or griddle pan. If using a griddle pan, rub 1 teaspoon of oil on the halloumi to stop it sticking. Fry for 2 minutes on each side until golden.

Arrange the halloumi on a serving dish, and top with the salsa. Finish with a generous sprinkling of pomegranate seeds.

Kofta kebab pitta with tomato and cucumber salad

Serves 4 (5 small koftas each)

For the koftas

500g lean beef mince

1 small red onion, chopped

1 teaspoon ground cumin

1 teaspoon paprika

½ teaspoon ground coriander

½ tablespoon peeled and grated ginger (approximately 25g)

4 tablespoons chopped fresh coriander

1 teaspoon fine salt

olive oil, for frying

4 pitta breads, halved

For the salad

1 large tomato, deseeded and chopped

1 small red onion, thinly sliced

½ cucumber, peeled, deseeded and thinly sliced

2 tablespoons roughly chopped flat leaf parsley

4 tablespoons olive oil

juice of 1 lemon

salt, to taste

To serve

Greek yoghurt

I love making koftas, be they fish, chicken, prawn or potato. There is something laborious and yet so satisfying about rolling the balls to exactly the right size . . . then cooking them and watching them slowly disappear as curious noses and sneaky little fingers crowd round. They are lightly spiced, great in the warm toasted pitta with the tomato and cucumber salad, and the yoghurt cools them down. These koftas are great made in a large batch and frozen, ready to be reheated for another day. Alternatively, any leftovers can be cooked into a curry – if they don't get eaten by the mysterious kofta-pinchers first.

Prep: 25 minutes   Cook: 20 minutes (2 batches, 10 minutes each)
❄: **Can be frozen**

To make the koftas: Combine the beef, red onion, cumin, paprika, ground coriander, ginger and fresh coriander in a bowl. Season generously with salt, and mix together by hand. Place in the fridge and leave to chill for 30 minutes.

Take the mixture out of the fridge, grease your hands with a little oil to stop the mixture sticking, and roll balls the size of whole walnuts in their shells.

Grill the koftas in a hot griddle pan or under the grill, turning them occasionally. They should take 10–12 minutes to cook.

To make the salad: Put all the salad ingredients into a bowl, adding the oil and lemon juice last and mixing well. Season well with salt and set aside until you are ready to serve.

To assemble: Cut a pitta in half and toast it. Open it up and fill it with a few koftas, along with some salad and dollop of Greek yoghurt.

Burnt garlic, chilli and lemon squid

Serves 5 as a starter, or as a small lunch with salad

This has to be the quickest recipe of all time. But don't be fooled by its speedy nature. It packs a punch, and if you're a squid lover like me this is the recipe for you. The chilli and lemon are almost an obvious choice for squid, but the burnt garlic takes the whole dish up a notch. The burning allows for some of the garlic flavour to come through combined with a heady dose of charring. Be sure not to overcook the squid, or it will become rubbery . . . and there's nothing worse than chewy squid.

4 whole squid with
  tentacles, cleaned
  (approximately 550g)

4 cloves of garlic

1 lemon, sliced into 8

2 tablespoons finely
  chopped coriander
  (a small packet)

2 spring onions,
  finely chopped

1 red chilli, finely chopped
  (deseeded for less heat)

salt, to taste

½ teaspoon pink
  peppercorns, crushed

3 tablespoons olive oil,
  for frying

Prep: 15 minutes Cook: **5 minutes** ❄: **Cannot be frozen**

Cut the squid into roughly similar-sized pieces, and score with a knife, making sure not to cut all the way through the flesh.

Put the garlic cloves in a heatproof glass or metal bowl. Blowtorch the cloves of garlic with the skins on until they are completely black. Chop the burnt garlic into small pieces, making sure not to discard any of the charred black bits, as they add to the flavour.

Add the lemon slices to the garlic, squeezing some juice out of each slice. Then add the coriander, spring onions, chilli, salt and pink peppercorns. Give everything a good stir.

Put a large frying pan over a medium heat and add the oil, then when the oil is hot add the squid. Stir, and after a few seconds add the rest of the spicy mix. Cook the squid for about 4 minutes. You will know when it is done when it curls up and looks less translucent.

A little bit of something sweet

So I am the kind of girl who, despite being in my (early!) thirties, still has stashes of sweets. If I were to admit to any kind of guilty pleasure, it would have to be sweeties. Boiled, cooked, whizzed, set, mixed . . . you name it, I am on it. I have stashes in my handbag, among my kitchen utensils, inside my kitchen roll, in my make-up drawer and even under my pillow. If there's a rustling of wrappers in the dark, that would be me having a sleepless night and trying to surreptitiously unwrap a cherry drop. To this day my kids haven't worked out where all my secret locations are, though I suppose they know now. (Mind you, there are a few places I won't admit to . . .) Anyway, they do know of my unhealthy obsession – one that has never left me, and probably never will.

Bubblegum marshmallow

Makes 40 squares

Marshmallow is a winner in our home. It's light, fluffy and doesn't feel unhealthy – though despite this, we do eat it in moderation. I love using homemade marshmallow in my baking. This marshmallow is bubblegum flavoured. It's juvenile, yes, but we all have a kid inside us somewhere, and the smell of bubblegum transports me to another time. The flavour may divide opinion, but it's one of my favourites. Feel free to use any essences or extracts you may have at home to vary the flavour, and experiment with different colours of sugar.

For the marshmallow

vegetable oil, for greasing

250ml water

30g powdered gelatine

300g granulated sugar

100ml liquid glucose

2 egg whites

a pinch of fine sea salt

2 drops bubblegum essence

For the coloured sugar

400g caster sugar

2 drops blue food colouring

2 drops bubblegum essence (or, if you're not a fan, orange, lemon or vanilla extract – the possibilities are endless)

Prep: 20 minutes, plus 2 hours for setting ❄: Cannot be frozen

Lightly grease 2 x 12-hole candy moulds, making sure you cover all the nooks and crannies. I prefer to use a mould that doesn't have too many indentations, and I think silicone moulds work best.

Put 100ml of the water in a bowl, and sprinkle over the gelatine. Leave it to soak for 5 minutes.

Put the granulated sugar, liquid glucose and the other 150ml of water in a saucepan over a high heat, and stir until the sugar has dissolved. Bring to the boil and keep boiling until the mixture reaches 121°C. Remove the pan from the heat, then add the soaked gelatine and mix it through.

Whisk the egg whites in a stand mixer or with a handheld mixer until you have soft peaks. Mix in the bubblegum essence. Continue to whisk, and slowly add the sugar and gelatine mixture. Keep whisking until the egg mixture has cooled and thickened.

Place the cooled meringue mixture into a piping bag, and pipe it into the greased moulds. Give the moulds a good slam on the work surface to get rid of any air bubbles.

To make the coloured sugar, mix together the caster sugar, food colouring and bubblegum essence in a ziplock bag. Seal it and mix the contents with your hands. Now sprinkle the coloured sugar on the bottoms of the marshmallows. Leave them to set for 2 hours, then gently remove them from the moulds. Roll the marshmallows in the remaining blue sugar.

The marshmallows can be stored in an airtight container for 2 weeks and they're perfect in rocky road, or melted between crackers.

Candied orange peel with dark and white chocolate

Makes 40 pieces

I only started making these because I can't bear to throw anything away. So when the kids would eat oranges and helpfully leave the peel lying around on the side, I would wash, de-pith and slice it – and turn what might otherwise have ended up in the bin into a little bit of candied peel goodness. These are chewy, sweet and zesty, and even better dipped in chocolate.

2 large oranges

250g caster sugar

50g white chocolate, melted

50g dark chocolate, melted

Prep: 30 minutes, plus cooling   Cook: 1 hour 20 minutes

Line a baking sheet with greaseproof paper.

Cut the oranges into quarters on the outside with a sharp knife. Make sure not to cut through the fruit completely – you just want to score the skin.

Peel the skin away with your fingers, then use the sharp knife to take off any white pith. Cut the skin into 1cm strips.

Put the strips of orange into a large pan with 250ml water over a high heat. Bring to the boil, then reduce the heat and simmer for 3 minutes. Drain the water.

Repeat the above process twice more, then set aside the peel, which should now be softer.

Place 500ml of water in a pan with the sugar. Boil until the sugar has completely dissolved, then add the softened orange peel, and reduce the heat to a gentle simmer. Leave simmering for 30–40 minutes, until the peel is tender and translucent.

Drain the peel well and put it on the lined baking sheet, then leave it to cool for a few hours, or as long as a day if you can, to dry completely.

Now the peel needs dipping in chocolate. Divide the peel into two batches. Dip one batch in the dark chocolate and the other batch in white chocolate.

Once set, these will keep in an airtight container for up to 1 month. These are great sprinkled on top of a buttery Madeira cake, or simply served after dinner as a sweet treat.

Chocolate-dipped honeycomb

Makes 30 pieces

You know that moment when you bite into a Crunchie bar as a child, look inside and ask yourself 'what kind of sorcery is this?' I learned very quickly that Crunchie was my husband's favourite chocolate bar – and as easy as it is to buy it from the shop, it's even easier to make, with no sorcery required. It's just honeycomb dipped in chocolate.

vegetable oil, for greasing

200g golden caster sugar

100ml runny honey

2 teaspoons bicarbonate of soda

100g dark chocolate (70% cocoa solids), melted

Prep: 10 minutes, plus cooling   Cook: 10 minutes

Line and grease a deep rectangular brownie tin right to the top so that the paper comes at least 3cm over the rim, as the honeycomb rises. Make sure the paper is greased liberally as this will help you remove the honeycomb once it has set.

Put the sugar and honey in a large, heavy-based saucepan over a medium heat until the sugar turns an amber colour. Make sure the sugar has all dissolved.

Remove the pan from the heat and stir in the bicarbonate of soda.

Pour the mixture into the prepared tin, and leave it to set for about 30 minutes.

Once the honeycomb has cooled, break it into uneven shards and dip the end of the honeycomb into the melted milk chocolate.

This can be eaten as it is, crumbled on top of ice cream, or baked into a brownie or cheesecake . . . the possibilities are endless. Or it can be stored in an airtight container for up to weeks as you eat your way through it.

Peanut, black sesame and ginger brittle

Makes 25 pieces

The first time I had peanut brittle was when my eldest sister, Jasmin, passed her GCSEs, and my dad's friend bought her this tiny, unassuming bag of peanut brittle tied up with maroon ribbon. The funny thing is she hates peanuts – in fact, she detests nuts of any kind – so it was a jackpot for the rest of us. We held back until my dad's friend left, but that was it. The peanut brittle was gone before he'd reached the front gate. (Bear in mind that we lived in a terraced house with a sliver of a front garden.) Then I didn't eat brittle again until I made it a few years ago – and this is my variation of the classic, with black sesame for added drama and nuttiness, and a hint of ginger.

vegetable oil, for greasing

150g raw skinned peanuts

50g black sesame seeds

3 pieces of candied ginger

¼ teaspoon ground ginger

300g caster sugar

Prep: 20 minutes   Cook: 20 minutes

Grease and line a 15 x 20cm tin with baking paper. Toast the peanuts in a non-stick pan, until they are golden. Put them in a bowl, and use the end of a rolling pin to crush them slightly.

Now toast the black sesame seeds for a few minutes in the same pan, being careful not to burn them. Mix them with the toasted peanuts, and leave them to cool.

Rinse the pieces of candied ginger and dry them on kitchen paper, then grate them finely. Add the grated ginger to the nut mixture and stir to combine, along with the ground ginger.

Now put the sugar in an even layer in a heavy-based pan, over a low–medium heat. Move the pan around now and again, but do not stir the sugar. The sugar will slowly turn a golden amber colour.

Once all the sugar is amber, add nuts, and pour everything into the prepared tin.

Leave it to stand for a few minutes, as the caramel will be really hot, then take a sharp knife and score where you would like to break the brittle. Once it has completely cooled, break it into pieces.

The brittle can be stored in a airtight container for up to 2 weeks. Sometimes I like to whizz it up in the food processer, and use it as a crunchy coating for chocolate truffles.

Mango fruit leather strips

Makes 20 strips

I used to watch my aunts make these on our travels to Bangladesh. Mangoes are literally everywhere in the Bengali summer. As they ripen there are new green ones to follow, and then there are the mangoes that have gone too far and ripened to the point where they are falling apart. But at this stage they are at their sweetest, and at their best for making these mango leather strips. They are cooked and then dried in the summer sun on the tin roofs. I don't have a tin roof or much sun, so this is my variation of a classic that reminds me of my childhood holidays. This recipe also works well with plums, apricots, peaches, raspberries and strawberries.

vegetable oil, for greasing

2 very ripe medium
  mangoes, peeled

40g caster sugar

juice of 1 lime

Prep: **20 minutes**   Cook: **approx 7 hours**

Very lightly grease a shallow Swiss roll tin (23cm x 33cm), line it with greaseproof paper, and very, very lightly grease the paper. You don't want so much grease that it starts to fry the mango.

Preheat the oven to 50°C/fan 30°C.

Cut off the mango flesh, and put it in a non-stick pan. Add the mango stones to the pan, too, and allow the pulp to be cooked off them.

Cook for 15 minutes over a low–medium heat. The fruit should become very soft and pulpy. Add it to a processor and whizz for 1 minute.

Put the mango back in the pan, and add the caster sugar and lime juice. Cook over a medium heat for 10 minutes, until the sugar has dissolved and the mixture has thickened. Take the pan off the heat and strain the mango through a sieve, removing all the lumps.

Put the mango paste into the prepared tin and, using an offset spatula, spread it out in a thin layer.

Bake for 7 hours. It might take longer if the mixture is spread thickly, and less time if the mixture is thinner. It will be ready when it's leathery to the touch and peels away from the base of the tin.

Once the leather is dry, cut it into strips. Roll it up tightly to store – it will keep for 2 weeks in an airtight container.

Tip: If you cannot find ripe-enough fresh mango, you can use two cans of drained ripe mango. I don't think it imparts the same flavour, but it still works.

Guava Turkish delight

Makes 36 squares

Just the thought of Turkish delight used to make my toes curl and my eyes water, perhaps because my abiding memory of it was the prepackaged stuff in purple cellophane. This Turkish not-so-delight was covered in a thin layer of chocolate, and the filling was gloopy and soft and tasted like my mum's incense. But I can't bear to hate any food – so I braved Turkish delight again 14 years later, when Abdal came home with some from a lads' holiday in Turkey. I was pleasantly surprised at the firmer texture, the subtle flavour and the light pink hue. I have since learned to love making my own Turkish delight in an array of flavours.

vegetable oil,
  for greasing

25g gelatine powder

250ml water

250ml guava juice

4 teaspoons guava syrup

1 teaspoon rose syrup

450g caster sugar

4 drops pink food
  colouring

6 tablespoons icing
  sugar, sifted

2 tablespoons cornflour,
  sifted

Prep: **15 minutes, plus 12 hours for setting time**
Cook: **10 minutes**   ❄: **Cannot be frozen**

Very lightly oil a 20cm square baking tin and line with clingfilm to help remove the turkish delight at the end. Add 20ml of the water to a bowl, sprinkle the gelatine on top and leave it to bloom for 5 minutes.

Put the remaining water, the guava syrup, rose syrup and caster sugar in a medium saucepan over a low heat, and stir until all the sugar has dissolved. Bring the mixture to the boil and reduce the heat.

Simmer for 20–25 minutes until the mixture thickens. Remove from the heat and allow to cool slightly before adding the gelatine and food colouring. Stir to combine and set aside for 10 minutes to cool further.

Pour the mixture into the prepared tin and leave it at room temperature for 12 hours.

Cut the Turkish delight into 2.5cm squares with a lightly greased knife. If you find that it sticks to the knife, grease the knife with flavourless oil. Mix the cornflour and icing sugar in a shallow bowl and use this to coat the Turkish delight.

It is now ready to eat, or it can stored in an airtight container between layers of greaseproof paper for up to 2 weeks.

Tip: I like to roll the Turkish delight in the mixture at least six times over a 24-hour period. I know this is laborious, but it gives it a lovely white coating that doesn't dissolve when the Turkish delight is left out. It's not a must.

Liquorice treacle toffees

Makes 36 squares

Almost nobody else in my family likes liquorice, so when I make these I make them all for myself. I make them, I store them, and I devour them . . . and occasionally, I fill my dad's pockets with them if he visits. He's the only other one who appreciates the flavour of this beautiful root. This toffee has a smokiness from the dark sugar, with the background flavour of liquorice.

300g dark brown
   soft sugar

80ml black treacle

50ml whole milk

50ml double cream

30g unsalted butter

4 drops liquorice oil
   or extract

1/8 teaspoon bicarbonate
   of soda

Prep: **10 minutes**   Cook: **20 minutes**   ❄: **Cannot be frozen**

Grease a deep baking tray (23cm x 33cm) and line it with baking paper, and very lightly grease the paper.

Put the sugar, treacle, milk, cream and butter in a heavy-based saucepan over a medium heat, and stir the mixture until the sugar has dissolved. Continue to heat until the mixture reaches 138°C – this will take about 20 minutes. Check using a thermometer.

Once it has reached temperature, add the liquorice oil or extract and the bicarbonate of soda. Mix it well to combine, and pour the toffee into the prepared tin.

After 5 minutes, snip the toffee into bite-sized pieces with a pair of kitchen scissors, and leave it to cool for at least 3 minutes. Don't leave it any longer than 5 minutes to cut the toffee as it will be too hard.

The toffee should keep for up to 4 weeks in an airtight container. I like to wrap it in individual pieces of greaseproof paper.

Rose, white chocolate and pistachio meringue kisses

Makes 44

I love making meringues, especially these little kisses. There is something quite soothing about piping rows of them to an exact size. The combination of rose pink with creamy white chocolate and vibrant purple and green crushed pistachios makes these both colourful and delicious. They're great for any occasion, and they are my favourite thing to wrap in cellophane, seal with matching ribbon and give out as a gift.

For the meringues

2 medium egg whites

⅛ teaspoon cream of tartar

110g caster sugar

½ teaspoon rose water

a few drops of pink food colouring

For the decoration

100g white chocolate, chopped

50g unsalted shelled pistachios

Prep: 25 minutes   Cook: 1 hour

Preheat the oven to 100°C/fan 80°C. Line two baking sheets with baking paper or silicone pads. Fit a piping bag with a large star-shaped nozzle. Line two trays with greaseproof paper.

Put the egg whites in a mixing bowl, and whisk until you have stiff peaks, then add the cream of tartar. Add the sugar a teaspoonful at a time, until all the sugar is incorporated. Now add the rose water and the pink food colouring, and mix thoroughly. The meringue mixture should now be glossy, shiny and thick.

Spoon the meringue into the piping bag, and pipe rosettes about 3cm wide. Leave a 2cm gap between the meringue kisses.

Bake in the oven for between 1 hour and 1 hour 15 minutes. The meringues should be dry to the touch and will come easily off the lining. Leave them to cool on a wire rack for a few minutes while you melt the white chocolate.

Melt the white chocolate in the microwave, or in a heat proof bowl over a pan of barely simmering water. Crush the pistachios to a fine powder in a food processor. Dip the bases of the meringues into the melted chocolate, and scrape off any excess. Now dip them in the crushed pistachios, and leave them to set on the prepared trays.

The meringue kisses can be stored in an airtight container for up to 1 week. They are beautiful tumbled in a jar and eaten when you need a sugar hit. I also like them to top a tall, naked cake.

Virgin mojito lollipops

Makes 10

Despite being a confectionery addict, I try my hardest not to allow the kids too much sugar. I have far more discipline where they are concerned. These, however, are a treat for the little ones as well as the adults – my take on one of my favourite mocktails: zesty lime, apple and mint lollies. Pure summer, in lollipop form, minus the sunhats.

100g caster sugar

250ml water

160ml golden syrup

3 tablespoons lime cordial

1 tablespoon apple cordial

zest of 1 lime

2 drops of peppermint essence

Prep: 15 minutes, plus 1 hour for hardening Cook: 25–30 minutes

Place 10 lollipop sticks on two greased baking sheets. I prefer to use silicone pads for extra insurance, but greaseproof paper will work just fine.

Place the sugar, water and golden syrup in a heavy-based pan. Bring to the boil, stirring all the time. Now leave the mixture over a medium to high heat for 25–30 minutes. There is no need to stir during this time.

Using a sugar thermometer check the temperature. Once it gets to 160°C add the lime and apple cordials, lime zest and peppermint essence. The cordials will cool the mixture down, so let the heat rise back up to 160°C then, leave the mixture in the pan for another 10 minutes, to thicken.

Now, using a tablespoon, spoon the mixture on to the lollipop sticks, and leave to harden for 1 hour. These lollipops keep for up to 1 week. They are great wrapped in cellophane and given to kids at a party.

Snacks & small plates

Savoury snacks and small plates of flavoursome goodness are never too far away from any of my family get-togethers. (A get-together can mean all twenty-three of us, or just my sisters popping over after doing their flat-pack furniture shopping.) When most people picture a cup of tea or coffee, they think biscuit or cake. Not where we are concerned, though – it's always a generous helping of something savoury, aromatic and warm, with lots of side plates for everyone to take their share and sit comfortably with their hot drink. (I like the spot near the radiator on the rocking chair.) So this savoury snack has become customary with our cup of tea. (And coffee, for the two family members who bizarrely prefer it; who are they, and are we really related?) It always begins with a simple 'What shall we have with our tea?' and ends with a flurry of suggestions. Whichever kind person offers to take on the task of cooking, it usually ends up being an excuse for my mum and her daughters to have a gossip about something, and us getting told off. That just makes the resulting snacks all the more tasty, as we catch each other's eye mid-bite and remember what we shouldn't have been speaking about.

Beetroot and mackerel crescents

Makes 25

This is one of my waste-not-want-not recipes. When mum went away on holiday, and I was looking after my brothers and sister, I was determined to use up every ingredient in my own house before I left. I found cooked beetroot in the fridge and a tin of mackerel, and packed them along with my kitchen sink. I came up with this blend of earthy, sweet, cooked beetroot paired with spices and deliciously rich, oily mackerel. The combination was so good my little sister still raves about it. She could easily do it herself, but she says it tastes better when I make it (perhaps a little work-shy). When you bite through the pastry, the colour inside is such a delight: vibrant and delicious.

For the filling

2 tablespoons vegetable oil

1 clove of garlic, crushed

½ small red onion, finely chopped

½ teaspoon salt

200g cooked beetroot, diced

100g tin mackerel

1 teaspoon ground cumin

a handful of dill, chopped

For the pastry

220g plain flour, plus extra for rolling

a pinch of fine sea salt

30ml vegetable oil, plus extra for frying

100–125ml warm water

Prep: **30 minutes, plus resting**   Cook: **25 minutes**
❄: **Can be frozen before frying if defrosted for 8 hours**

To make the filling: Put the oil in a frying pan over a medium heat, then add the garlic, red onion and salt and cook for 5 minutes, until starting to soften.

Now add the beetroot, mackerel and cumin, stir to combine, and cook for a further 10 minutes. Take the mixture off the heat and stir in the chopped dill.

To make the pastry: Put the flour and salt in a bowl. Add the oil and rub it in, until you have a loose, crumbly mixture.

Add the water a little at a time, and bring the dough together with your hands. This should take about 5 minutes. Wrap the dough in clingfilm, and set it aside for 30 minutes at room temperature. (Put it in the fridge if the dough is very soft.)

Roll out the pastry to 2mm thickness on a floured surface, and cut circles about 8cm in diameter. Place a teaspoon of the cooled filling in the centre of each circle, and pinch the edges together to create a decorative border, using your fingers or a fork.

Heat 1cm oil in a frying pan, and fry the crescents in 2–3 batches for a few minutes on each side, until golden. Drain on kitchen paper and then serve.

Tip: There is always a little bit of filling left over, so I usually save this and mix it with pasta for my husband's lunch. I like making too much filling and finding another use for it. Any leftover filling can be eaten with rice as a main meal or frozen to make more pastries.

Aromatic spiced salmon balls

Makes 20 balls

My love of seafood is probably quite apparent, but it is such a versatile ingredient, takes on flavour so well and is, thankfully, readily available. These spiced balls are great as a snack, and even better served with a dip. The coriander adds freshness to the whole thing. It's great with a squeeze of lemon before serving, too.

1 slice of bread

500g raw salmon fillets, skins removed, roughly chopped

1 teaspoon ground cumin

1 teaspoon turmeric

3 cloves of garlic, crushed

1 medium egg

40g breadcrumbs

zest of 1 lemon (cut into wedges to serve with the balls)

1 tablespoon fresh coriander, chopped

salt, to taste

plain flour, for dusting

vegetable oil, for frying

Prep: 30 minutes   Cook: 5 minutes per batch   ❄: Can be frozen

Soak the slice of bread in water, squeeze out the excess and put the bread in a food processor. (There is nothing weirder than soaking bread in water.)

Add the salmon, cumin, turmeric, garlic, egg, breadcrumbs, lemon zest and coriander to the food processor. Season generously with salt, then blitz until the mixture comes together. Leave in the fridge for half an hour.

Take the chilled mixture out of the fridge, and roll it into 2.5cm balls.

Put the flour on a large plate. Roll each ball in the flour, and dust off any excess.

Heat the vegetable oil in a large frying pan, and fry the balls for about 5 minutes. You may need to do this in two batches. Alternatively, you could bake the balls on a parchment-lined tray for 15–20 minutes at 180°C/fan 160°C.

Drain the balls on kitchen paper, and serve.

Can be frozen before or after frying; if before, defrost in the fridge for 8 hours, then cook as in the recipe.

Cheese and chive popcorn

Serves 4

Popcorn is very up-and-coming, and there are so many variations to try. What used to be simply salty or sweet now comes in the most fascinating flavours. Popcorn is a cheap and healthy snack that is easy to make and store at home – so much ease, and so little effort. This recipe is really easy, and quite delicious if I may say so myself. Once the corn is popped, the addition of the Parmesan gives it seasoning as well as flavour. The chives add a hint of onion without being overwhelming. You can experiment with the kind of cheese you use, and the herbs. Popcorn is a blank canvas that takes almost any flavour really well.

2 tablespoons vegetable oil

100g popcorn kernels

30g Parmesan cheese, finely grated

a large handful of finely chopped chives

salt and freshly ground black pepper, to taste

Prep: **5 minutes**   Cook: **5 minutes**

Heat the oil over a high heat in a large pan that has a lid.

Put in the popcorn kernels, and stir well. Turn down the heat and put the lid on.

You will hear the kernels start to pop slowly, then more rapidly, then they will slow down again. Make sure to give the pan a shake every few minutes while they are popping. Once the popping has stopped, take the pan off the heat and remove the lid.

Tip the popcorn out into a bowl, and add the Parmesan, chives, salt and a generous sprinkling of black pepper.

Crispy taco chicken salsa cups

Makes: 6

These crispy cups are so easy to make and I have been known to fill them with anything that they are willing to hold, whether it's this combination of shredded chicken and salsa, or all sorts of other delights. Just don't do what my daughter does and use it as a cup to drink water with, unless it's a monumental mess you are looking for, in which case, go ahead.

For the chicken breast

2 skinless chicken breasts

1 tablespoon vegetable oil

fine sea salt and crushed black pepper to taste

For the taco cups

6 large tortillas

6 tablespoons olive oil

For the salsa

1 green chilli, finely chopped, seeds removed (or keep the seeds if you're feeling adventurous)

1 garlic clove, crushed

1 large green pepper

2 spring onions, roughly chopped

1 tablespoon white vinegar or cider vinegar

a handful of coriander, chopped roughly

salt and freshly ground black pepper, to taste

sour cream, to serve

Prep: **30 minutes**   Cook: **40 minutes**

For the chicken: Preheat the oven to 180°C/fan 160°C. Put the chicken on a non-stick small roasting tin. Drizzle with oil, season and cover with foil. Bake in oven for 20–25 mins until cooked through.

Once the chicken is cooked, shred it using 2 forks and season with salt and pepper.

For the taco cups: Preheat the oven to 200°C/fan 180°C and have your 6-hole muffin tray at the ready. Brush each wrap with oil on both sides and push into the muffin tray, tucking it in where necessary to keep it in place.

Line each cup with a little baking paper square and fill with baking beads, just to weight them down, they have a habit of just flying out.

Place the tray in the oven for 10-15 minutes, until the cups are golden and crisp. Take them out and leave to cool in the tray.

For the salsa: if you are using a food processor then roughly chop the ingredients and give them a quick blitz to give you a rough salsa – be careful not to liquidize though. I like to chop everything individually as this stops all the juices from being released.

Add salt and pepper to taste.

To serve, place some chicken into each cup and top with the salsa and some sour cream, if you like.

Curried chicken liver pâté

Serves 4

It was only after we got married that I realized my husband and I were two very different people in terms of taste. He likes safe and easy, and I like unusual and complicated. For example, I love chicken livers: grilled, curried, pâtéd . . . They're cheap, and an amazing source of iron – the kind of food that we grew up on as children. One day I was cooking up chicken liver curry for my own kids, realised I'd bought a little too much liver, and looked up a recipe for chicken liver pâté. I was hopeful of converting my husband into a chicken liver fan, but he took one taste and turned his nose up at it yet again. On a mission now, I came up with this curried version. The curry powder is just enough to give the pâté a subtle aroma, and at last, even though my husband still only eats chicken livers in pâté form, I was able to change his mind. This pâté pairs well with crusty bread, vegetable sticks or pitta chips. I love eating it with any store-bought sweet lime pickle.

100g salted butter

1 small onion, finely chopped

2 cloves of garlic, crushed

2 bay leaves

225g chicken livers, trimmed and cleaned

2 teaspoons mild curry powder

1 anchovy fillet

salt and freshly ground black pepper, to taste

150g unsalted butter, for topping

Prep: 15 minutes   Cook: 20 minutes, plus cooling
Will keep for up to 1 week covered in the fridge,
as long as the seal of clarified butter is intact

To make the pâté: Put the salted butter in a medium frying pan over a medium heat. Add the onion, garlic and bay leaves. Give everything a good mix, and cook for 5–10 minutes.

Now add the chicken livers and the curry powder. Cook the livers for about 5 minutes, leaving them slightly pink in the middle. Add the salt and pepper.

Leave the mixture to cool for about 10 minutes. Take out the bay leaves and discard them.

Whizz everything in a blender with the anchovy until you have a smooth paste. Pass the pâté through a sieve to get rid of any lumps. Divide the mixture between 4 ramekins.

To make the clarified butter topping: Put the unsalted butter in a small saucepan and bring it to the boil. Once it has boiled, take it off the heat and set it aside.

There should be a white froth on top of the melted butter. Carefully remove the froth, leaving the clear butter underneath. Leave to cool, then gently pour the clear melted butter on top of the pâté in the ramekins, and leave in the fridge for a few hours to set before serving.

This is best served with crusty bread and lime pickle.

Easy aromatic meat samosas

Makes 16

Samosas are a staple in any Bengali diet. They are almost always made in enormous batches then frozen ready for any time we all get together for a catch-up. This recipe is great, because you don't have to worry about making pastry – the tortilla makes a fantastic shell for the aromatic mince filling to call home. Once fried, it becomes crisp on the outside but still maintains a slight chewiness.

For the filling

450g lean lamb mince

5 cloves of garlic, crushed

8cm piece of ginger, peeled and finely grated

2 teaspoons garam masala

1 teaspoon cumin seeds

2 green chillies, finely chopped (deseeded for less heat)

½ teaspoon chilli flakes

½ teaspoon chilli powder

1 teaspoon fine sea salt

225g potatoes, peeled and diced into ½cm cubes

125g frozen peas

large handful of fresh coriander, chopped

For the 'pastry'

8 flour tortillas

1 large egg, beaten

vegetable oil, for frying

Prep: 20 minutes, plus cooling   Cook: 45 minutes   ❄: Can be frozen (before shallow frying); defrost in fridge for 8 hours before frying

To make the filling: Fry the mince in a large pan over a high heat for 5 minutes, until browned.

Now add the garlic, ginger, garam masala, cumin seeds, chilli flakes and powder, salt and potatoes. Cook, covered, over a medium heat for 15 minutes, stirring occasionally. Until all the moisture has been absorbed.

Add the peas and cook for further 10 minutes over a very low heat, until the potatoes are cooked through. If the potatoes start to stick to the pan, add a small splash of water.

Take the pan off the heat and allow the mixture to cool completely. Add the chopped coriander, and stir it through. At this stage you can keep the mixture in the fridge for a day or two, until you are ready to make the samosas.

To assemble the samosa: Cut the tortillas in half. Add samosa mix to the centre of each half, and brush the edges with a little egg. Bring the flat edge together to make a triangular shape, fill and hold the rounded end together until it sticks firmly in place.

Put 1cm of oil in a large frying pan over a medium-high heat and shallow fry the samosas in batches for 1–2 minutes on each side, until golden brown and heated through, then drain on kitchen paper. Or, for a healthier option, you can brush the samosas with a little oil and bake them in a preheated oven at 180°C/fan 160°C for 15 minutes.

Tip: I deliberately make a really generous amount of mixture. Add a can of chopped tomatoes and heat for 15 minutes over a medium heat to make enough Bolognese for three little kids the next day.

Garlic and parsley breadsticks

Makes 24

Breadsticks are a great way to get started using yeast, without diving straight into making bread. You know exactly what to aim for when making them: a crisp snap, and a golden-brown colour. These have a great garlic flavour, and the parsley just adds specks of green, making them look and taste delightful. You can alter the spices – try paprika or onion seeds. You can also use different dried herbs, like chives or thyme. The world is your breadstick where flavouring is concerned.

500g strong white bread flour

7g fast-action yeast

1 teaspoon sugar

1 teaspoon salt

1 tablespoon olive oil, plus extra for surface

4 teaspoons dried parsley

3 teaspoons garlic powder

280ml water

Prep: **25 minutes, plus rising**   Cook: **20 minutes**
❄: **Can be frozen**

Put the flour in a mixing bowl, then add the yeast on one side and the sugar and salt on the other.

Now add the olive oil, dried parsley and garlic powder. Stir everything together and make a well in the middle.

Gradually add the water, bringing the mixture together with your hands until a dough is formed. You may not need all the water.

If you are using a stand mixer, attach a dough hook and mix for 6 minutes. If you are kneading by hand, lightly oil the work surface and knead for 10 minutes, until the dough is smooth and elastic.

Lightly oil a bowl, put the dough in it, and leave it to prove for 1 hour, or until it has doubled in size.

Line two baking sheets with greaseproof paper or silicone pads.

Knock back the dough, then put it on a floured surface and roll out a rectangle approximately 25 x 40cm, and ½cm thick. Cut into 24 strips and place on the baking sheets.

Preheat the oven to 190°C/fan 170°C.

Meanwhile, put the breadsticks on the baking sheets inside clean bin liners, and leave to prove for 30 minutes.

Bake the breadsticks for 15–20 minutes, until they are golden brown.

Leave them to cool, and remove them from the baking sheets after 15 minutes. I like them slightly bready – they're perfect to eat with hummus or roasted red pepper dip. If you want a crunchier texture, bake for an additional 10 minutes.

Goat's cheese and black pepper puffs

Makes 24

These goat's cheese and black pepper puffs are very similar to a classic choux pastry . . . but this is the savoury version. I'm battling to decide which I prefer – I may have to get my pros and cons chart out to decide. They are very different from the sweet ones, but equally good in their own right. The goat's cheese provides saltiness (there's no need to add more salt) along with its distinctive flavour. But here the black pepper is the real star, its fragrance and warmth amplified by the goat's cheese. Together the two make for a delicious savoury treat that can be eaten as a snack, served as a canapé, or frozen to reheat at a later date.

75g unsalted butter

1 teaspoon fine sea salt

1 teaspoon freshly ground black pepper

150g plain flour, sifted

4 medium eggs, lightly beaten

100g hard goat's cheese, finely grated

Prep: 20 minutes **Cook:** 25 minutes ❄: Can be frozen

Preheat the oven to 220°C/fan 200°C. Line two large baking sheets with greaseproof paper.

Bring 250ml water to the boil in a large saucepan. Add the butter, salt and pepper. When the butter has melted, take the pan off the heat.

Add the flour quickly, and stir with a wooden spoon until you have a smooth, even paste that comes away from the sides of the pan.

Allow the mixture to cool for 5 minutes, then gradually add the egg, beating well between each addition. You may not need to use all the egg – you want a glossy paste that will drop from the spoon if you gently shake it. If the mixture is too thick, it won't puff up very much as it bakes; too runny, and it will spread rather than rise.

Finally, stir in the grated goat's cheese.

Spoon teaspoons of mixture on to the prepared baking trays, leaving 2.5cm between the puffs, to allow for expansion as they cook.

Bake at 220°C/fan 200°C for 10 minutes, and then lower the temperature to 200°C/fan 180°C before baking for a further 10–15 minutes.

The puffs are best served warm – you can make them up to 4 hours in advance, then reheat at 180°C/fan 160°C for 5–10 minutes to serve.

Kidney bean falafels with a coriander yoghurt dip

Makes 6

We have all heard of falafel made with chickpeas, and I often make them that way myself. But I came up with this recipe after finding twelve cans of kidney beans on offer for £4. My eagerness to grab a bargain meant I ended up with twenty-four cans lying around, and kids who were getting fed up of 'kidney beans with everything' month. I needed a way to disguise them and this worked brilliantly – the falafel still has the distinct taste of cumin, but with a very different texture. The kidney beans lose their stringy exterior, and are equally delicious. So if you have a load of canned beans you bought on offer, and a family threatening to walk out if you present them with the same thing yet again . . . try this!

For the falafels

2 tablespoons vegetable oil

3 garlic cloves, crushed

1 small onion, chopped

1 teaspoon fine sea salt

400g can red kidney beans, drained and rinsed

1 teaspoon cumin

1 teaspoon paprika

1 teaspoon ground coriander

a large handful of fresh coriander, chopped

1 medium egg, beaten

4 tablespoons chickpea flour

For the coriander and yoghurt dip

200ml Greek yoghurt

a large handful of fresh coriander, chopped roughly

3 cloves of garlic, peeled

a large pinch of salt

a squeeze of lemon juice

Prep: 15 minutes   **Cook:** 15 minutes if frying, 30 minutes if baking
❄: Can be frozen before frying

Heat 1 tablespoon oil in a small saucepan over a low to medium heat. Add the garlic, onion and salt, and cook for about 10 minutes, until soft. Tip everything into a large mixing bowl, and leave to cool.

Add the kidney beans, cumin, paprika, ground coriander, fresh coriander and egg to the bowl. Use a potato masher or food processor to mix thoroughly. The texture should be chunky but still hold its shape. Finally, add the chickpea flour, which will make the mixture a little drier.

Mould the mixture into six patties about 4cm diameter x 1cm deep. If the mixture is sticky and difficult to handle, you can lightly moisten your hands with oil or water. Alternatively, add a little more chickpea flour.

Heat 1 tablespoon oil in a large non-stick frying pan over a medium heat, and cook the falafels for 5 minutes on each side, pushing them down slightly with the back of a spatula to help them cook through.

For a healthier option, the falafels can also be baked in a preheated oven at 200°C/fan 180°C for 30 minutes.

Put all the ingredients for the dip into a food processor and blitz until the mixture is a bright, bold green.

Spiced pecan and mango trail mix

Serves 8 as a snack

Trail mix is an essential in our home. It's in the cupboards, in jars all over the place, and in packets in my handbags for emergency snack situations when we are on the go. Whenever I hear 'Mum, I'm hungry' – in the middle of shopping, when I'm trying to decide whether to buy two pairs of shoes or one, or just the handbag I saw 18 shops away – trail mix is a saviour. The spiced pecans are great; substantial enough that we don't go through them too quickly. With the hint of tang from the mango powder and the sweetness of the raisins, the balance is just right. Perfect with a drink, hot or cold.

1 tablespoon olive oil

1 teaspoon ground cumin

1 teaspoon ground coriander

½ teaspoon ground turmeric

1 tablespoon mango powder (amchoor powder)

300g pecans

1 teaspoon onion salt

1 teaspoon chilli flakes

a large handful of fresh coriander, chopped

a bunch of spring onions, finely chopped

100g raisins

Prep: **10 minutes**   Cook: **20 minutes**
Toasted nuts can be kept for up to 1 week in an airtight container.

Preheat the oven to 180°C/fan 160°C.

Put all the ingredients in a bowl, except for the fresh coriander, spring onions and raisins. Mix everything together, then spread it out on a baking sheet.

Bake for 20 minutes, stirring after the first 10 minutes. You will know when they are done when the spices attach themselves to the pecans, but be sure to keep an eye, on them in case they burn.

Once out of the oven, leave the mixture to cool completely on the baking sheet.

Once it's cooled, add the coriander and the spring onions, then the raisins. Toss everything together, and serve.

Wellington sausage rolls

Makes 25–30

Sausages are my guilty pleasure. I hate admitting it, but I love sausages – there, I said it! Wrapped in flaky puff pastry, surely they're every girl's secret dream (apart from a cappuccino-skinned hottie, which is every girl's other secret dream)? Anyway, these are my beef Wellington sausage rolls. The mushrooms mixed with the sausage make for a darker, meatier flavour. The layer of English mustard gives the sausage rolls a subtle heat once cooked. These are always a winner at kids' parties, and are even better when they end up in the packed lunch the next day. They freeze really well, so they can be popped in the oven as and when you need them.

30g unsalted butter

100g mushrooms, finely chopped

1 tablespoon Worcestershire sauce

1 tablespoon Tabasco, or less if you prefer, depending on your tolerance for heat

6 large beef sausages, taken out of the skins

a pinch of fine sea salt

freshly ground black pepper

plain flour, for dusting

450g puff pastry (shop-bought, or you can make your own)

4 tablespoons wholegrain mustard

1 medium egg, beaten

sea salt flakes, to sprinkle

Prep: **20 minutes**　Cook: **25 minutes**

❄. **Can be frozen before or after baking**

Preheat the oven to 200°C/fan 180°C.

Put the butter and the mushrooms in a small frying pan over a medium heat, and cook the mushrooms until they are soft and any moisture has evaporated. Put them in a bowl and leave to cool completely.

Once the mushrooms have cooled, add the Worcestershire sauce, Tabasco, sausagemeat, salt and pepper. Give everything a good mix by hand, and set aside.

Dust your surface with flour and roll the puff pastry out into a long wide rectangle approximately 25 x 35cm. Then cut down the middle lengthways to give you three long rectangles.

Brush the pastry rectangles with a generous layer of wholegrain mustard, making sure to leave a gap of 1cm along the long edges. Brush the exposed edges with the beaten egg.

Down the centre of the pastry rectangles, lay out a generous line of sausagemeat. Encase the filling with the pastry, making a seam joined with egg wash, underneath the roll.

Brush the three rolls in egg wash, and give them a light sprinkling of sea salt flakes. Cut each long roll into 8–10 pieces.

Place the small rolls on a baking sheet and bake for 15–20 minutes, until golden on the outside, making sure the meat on the inside is cooked through.

Za'atar and lemon palmiers

Makes: 18–20

Palmiers – or elephant's ears – are usually assumed to be sweet flaky biscuits made with puff pastry. But this savoury version is filled with a tangy thyme-like Lebanese spice called za'atar and lemon zest, then topped with an egg wash and sprinkled with sesame seeds. These play with your mind, because the shape suggests it will be sweet, but the taste says otherwise. Like magic, through cookery.

500g puff pastry (shop-bought, or you can make your own)

plain flour, for dusting

50g za'atar

zest of 2 lemons

1 medium egg, beaten

50g sesame seeds

Prep: **15 minutes, plus 30 minutes chilling** Cook: **15 minutes**
❄: **Can be frozen before baking (if you did not use frozen pastry)**

Roll out the puff pastry on a floured surface, to a 30 x 35cm rectangle the thickness of a pound coin.

Put the pastry on a baking sheet – this will make it easier to move when it has been rolled up.

Spread the whole rectangle of pastry with the za'atar, making sure to firmly press the spice into the dough. Now sprinkle the lemon zest all over the pastry, distributing it as evenly as you can.

With a short end towards you, roll the two long edges of the pastry inwards. Where the two rolls meet in the middle, brush the join lightly with the egg.

Put the whole thing in the fridge to chill for 30 minutes.

Preheat the oven to 200°C/fan 180°C. Line two baking sheets with greaseproof paper.

After 30 minutes remove the roll from the fridge and, using a sharp knife, cut it into slices about 1cm thick.

Lay the palmiers flat on the baking sheets, brush them with egg and sprinkle over the sesame seeds. Bake for 15 minutes, until light, golden and slightly puffy.

Leave the palmiers to cool on the baking sheets for 15 minutes before moving them to a cooling rack to cool completely.

Who stole the biscuits from the biscuit jar?

Biscuits were not an area I ventured into until a few years ago, when I discovered how many different types there actually are, and the myriad techniques involved in making and baking them. And so my biscuit journey began. We never baked at home when I was small, so I was all too familiar with shop-bought varieties like bourbons, custard creams, Nice biscuits, malted milks, and so on . . . you get the picture. Biscuits are a wonderful part of our heritage, and we British folk seem rather passionate about them, if not a little obsessed: everyone has their favourite, and everyone has their least favourite. Everyone has their own way of eating them. The all-in-oners, the nibblers, the dunkers, the forensic decapitators. Personally I'm a bit of everything, depending on what I'm having. So biscuits can be varied and versatile. They might be a treat after a meal, a quick snack to stave off hunger, a bite on the road, or prettily wrapped up as a way to say I'm thinking about you. At home we have a big cookie jar to help ourselves from, and refill it as we go.

Candied lemon peel cookies

Makes 40

These cookies are among my favourites to make. They are easy, and you can replace the lemon with whatever you may have in the cupboard – stem ginger, glacé cherries, prunes, mixed peel, currants . . . or you can simply leave them plain. The dough is wrapped neatly into a large sausage, chilled and then sliced. I freeze the dough ready to be sliced from semi-frozen, and I can have homemade warm biscuits on the table almost before the doorbell's stopped ringing. Now if that's not a treat for guests along with a fresh pot of tea, I don't know what is.

225g unsalted butter, softened

125g icing sugar

2 medium egg yolks

1 teaspoon Sicilian lemon extract

zest of 1 lemon

300g plain flour, sifted, plus extra for dusting

a pinch of fine sea salt

100g candied lemon peel, roughly chopped

Prep: **15 minutes**   Cook: **12 minutes**   Freezing time: **2 hours**
❄: **Dough can be frozen**

Cream the butter and icing sugar with a handheld mixer or a wooden spoon, until the mixture is light and fluffy.

Add the egg yolks one at a time, mixing to incorporate after each addition. Now add the lemon extract and zest, flour and salt.

Add the candied lemon peel, and mix everything together to form a dough.

Now divide the mixture in two and, on a floured surface, roll out the two pieces of dough into sausage shapes. Each should be about 5cm in diameter.

Wrap the dough sausages tightly in clingfilm, twisting the ends like a sweet wrapper to secure them. Freeze for at least 2 hours.

Preheat the oven to 180°C/fan 160°C. Line two baking sheets with greaseproof paper.

Cut the frozen cookie dough 'logs' into ½cm slices. Bake for 12 minutes, until they are golden brown.

Leave the cookies to cool on the baking sheet for 10 minutes before transferring to a wire rack to cool completely.

Cheese and tomato pizza rainbows

Makes 40

These savoury biscuits are so easy to make and even easier to eat. They have a crispy short texture, with all the flavour of pizza.

For the biscuits

150g plain flour, sieved

a pinch of fine sea salt

50g Cheddar cheese, finely grated

100g salted butter

1 egg, separated

1 tablespoon double-concentrated tomato purée

1 teaspoon dried oregano

1 teaspoon cracked black pepper

For the filling

3 tablespoons double-concentrated tomato purée

1 teaspoon dried oregano

1 teaspoon paprika

Prep: 20 minutes   Cook: 20 minutes

❄: Dough can be frozen as a log or once sliced

Put the flour, salt, cheese and butter in the food processor. Whizz until the ingredients come together to form a dough. Or you could do this by hand and rub all the ingredients together to a crumbly texture. Now add the tomato purée, oregano and black pepper and mix together to incorporate well. To this add the beaten egg yolk, which should just bring the dough together. If you are doing this by hand, be sure not to overwork.

Place the dough between two sheets of clingfilm, and roll it into a rectangular sheet about ½cm thick. Take off the top layer of clingfilm.

To make the filling, mix together the tomato purée, oregano and paprika. Spread the filling all over the biscuit dough.

With a long edge close to you, roll the dough up into a spiral. Wrap tightly in clingfilm, and refrigerate for 2 hours.

Preheat the oven to 200°C/fan 180°C. Line two baking sheets with baking paper.

Take the biscuit dough out of the fridge, remove the clingfilm and cut into slices about ½cm thick, then cut them in half. Place the biscuits on the baking sheets a few centimetres apart. Put them in the fridge for 10 minutes, then bake for 15–20 minutes. Leave the biscuits to cool on the baking sheets for 10 minutes, then move them to a wire rack to cool completely.

I call these biscuits. My kids call them pizza rainbows. I like pizza rainbows better.

Cherry Bakewell macaroons

Makes 6

These very English macaroons are a favourite. They are a lot less complicated to make then their French macaron counterparts, and equally (if not more) delicious. Here are the classic flavours of a Bakewell tart in the shell of a macaroon . . . moreish to say the least.

For the macaroons

2 sheets of rice paper

2 medium egg whites

¼ teaspoon cream of tartar

¼ teaspoon cornflour

140g caster sugar

225g desiccated coconut

1 teaspoon almond extract

¼ teaspoon fine sea salt

6 glacé cherries

For the topping

50g dark chocolate (70%), melted

50g flaked almonds, slivered and toasted

Prep: **15 minutes**   Cook: **20 minutes**   ❄: **Cannot be frozen**

Preheat the oven to 170°C/fan 150°C. Line a baking tray with greaseproof paper or silicone pads, and place the rice paper on top.

Whisk the egg whites, cream of tartar and cornflour until you have soft peaks. Now add a tablespoonful of sugar at a time, continuing to whisk, until the mixture becomes glossy – you should now have stiff peaks.

Now add the coconut, almond extract and salt, and fold in using a large metal spoon.

Place 6 large dollops of the mixture on the rice paper, spacing them 2cms apart. Press a glacé cherry into the centre of each macaroon.

Bake for 20 minutes, until the macaroons are golden brown and dry to the touch. Leave them to cool on the baking sheet for 15 minutes.

Carefully cut around each macaroon to remove the excess rice paper and drizzle each one with melted dark chocolate. Sprinkle over the toasted almonds.

Coconut and strawberry Anzacs

Makes 25

These delicious biscuits are named after the soldiers from Australia and New Zealand to whom they were sent in the First World War. They were originally made without egg so they could withstand travel. This recipe does contain an egg, which adds richness – seeing as they don't really need to travel overseas, why not? These alternative Anzacs contain freeze-dried strawberries, giving them a slight tartness and making them a little bit different.

85g porridge oats

85g desiccated coconut

100g plain flour

100g freeze-dried strawberries, broken into small pieces

100g caster sugar

150g unsalted butter

1 tablespoon golden syrup

1 teaspoon bicarbonate of soda

Prep: 10 minutes   Cook: 12–15 minutes   ❄: Cannot be frozen

Preheat the oven to 180°C/fan 160°C. Line two baking sheets with greaseproof paper.

Put the oats, coconut, flour, strawberries and sugar in a bowl, and stir to combine. Make a well in the centre.

Melt the butter in a small pan with the golden syrup and bicarbonate of soda, then add it to the dry mixture. Mix everything together thoroughly.

Put heaped tablespoons of the mix on to the prepared baking sheets, making sure the biscuits are about 4cm apart.

Bake for 12–15 minutes, until the biscuits are golden.

Leave them on the tray for 10 minutes to cool, then transfer to a wire rack to cool completely.

Fruit cake flapjacks

Makes 12

I love, love, love, fruit cake, but we always seem to have so much of it left over during the holiday season, especially around Easter and Christmas. So I have devised many ways of using up the spare cake, because if there's one thing I despise, it's waste. Here, the fruit cake adds some moisture as well as flavour, so these keep really well in a jar ready for packed lunches and picnics. You can use leftover simnel cake, too.

For the flapjacks

115g unsalted butter

55g soft light
  brown sugar

115g golden syrup

175g rolled oats

165g leftover fruit
  cake, crumbled

zest of 1 orange

For the topping

200g white chocolate,
  melted

a little orange zest

Prep: **15 minutes**   Cook: **35 minutes**   ❄: **Cannot be frozen**

Preheat the oven to 180°C/fan 160°C. Grease and line an 18cm square tin.

Gently heat the butter, sugar and golden syrup in a large saucepan, until the sugar has melted. Stir in the oats, crumbled fruit cake and orange zest. Mix until well combined.

Spread the mixture in the tin, and flatten the top.

Bake for 30–35 minutes until they are golden all over and slightly darker round the edges.

Take the flapjack out of the oven and cut it into slices, but leave it to cool completely in the tin.

Once cool, cover the whole flapjack with the melted white chocolate and leave to set. Sprinkle with orange zest before serving.

Chocolate and date cakey cookies

Makes 18–20

These cookies are dense and fudgy, and very chocolatey – this cannot be denied. They are great eaten straight away, which is usually the case in our home. Once cooled, they have the look of a biscuit but the texture of a brownie.

100g milk chocolate, broken into pieces

150g dark chocolate (70% cocoa solids), broken into pieces

75g unsalted butter

180g soft light brown sugar

3 medium eggs

1 teaspoon vanilla extract

130g plain flour, sifted, plus extra for dusting

1 teaspoon cinnamon

½ teaspoon fine sea salt

120g dates, roughly chopped and rolled in 1 tablespoon plain flour to keep them from sinking in the cookie

Prep: **25 minutes**   Cook: **10 minutes**   ❄: **Cannot be frozen**

Melt the milk and dark chocolate and the butter in the microwave or over a pan of barely simmering water, and mix together to incorporate. Set aside and leave the mixture to cool.

Put the brown sugar and eggs in a stand mixer, and beat together for 3 minutes at a medium speed (or use a handheld mixer).

Now add the chocolate and butter mixture, and continue to mix at a medium speed for 3 minutes.

Add the vanilla extract and mix it in.

Finally, add the flour, cinnamon, salt and chopped dates, and mix everything through with a large metal spoon.

The mixture will be quite runny, so leave it in the fridge for 15 minutes to firm up slightly.

Meanwhile, preheat the oven to 190°C/fan 170°C and line two baking sheets with baking paper or silicone pads, and lightly dust the surface with plain flour.

Using a medium ice cream scoop or 2 tablespoons, scoop the mix on to the prepared baking sheets, making 18–20 mounds. Don't be tempted to flatten them at this point, they bake best in mounds. Space them apart evenly, allowing for them to spread a little bit while baking.

Place in the fridge for 20 minutes to chill.

Bake for 10 minutes. They should be slightly cracked on the surface and look dry.

Leave the cookies to cool completely on the sheets before serving. These will keep for about 7 days in an airtight container.

Grapefruit cats' tongues

Makes 25

We're not baking actual cats' tongues . . . we're baking biscuits that look like them. But I still find it quite amusing when the kids ask, 'Mum, can we bake cats' tongues?' These biscuits are crisp and wafer-thin, and they go really well with a cup of tea as well as creamy desserts such as crème brûlées or crèma Catalanas. These are a little bit different, as they are flavoured with the zest of grapefruit, giving them an amazing flavour and zing.

125g unsalted butter, softened

125g icing sugar, sifted

zest of 1 grapefruit

3 egg whites

140g plain flour

a pinch of fine sea salt

Prep: **15 minutes**   Cook: **10 minutes**   ❄: **Cannot be frozen**

Preheat the oven to 180°C/fan 160°C, and line two baking sheets with greaseproof paper or silicone pads.

Cream the butter and the icing sugar together until the mixture is light and fluffy.

Now mix the grapefruit zest through.

Add the egg whites one at a time, and mix them through with a wooden spoon.

Finally, add the flour and salt and mix until you have a smooth batter.

Fit a large piping bag with a straight-edged 1cm nozzle. Pipe 25 lines about 8cm long and 2.5cm apart; the biscuits will spread as they bake.

Bake on the middle shelf for 10 minutes, until the biscuits are golden brown around the edge and set in the centre.

Leave to cool on the baking sheets for about 3 minutes, then transfer to a wire rack to cool completely.

Ovaltine bedtime biccies

Makes 35

These biscuits are malty, sweet and creamy, and the perfect bedtime snack with a glass of milk, for children and grown-ups alike. And they are great in packed lunches, too! They keep well in a sealed biscuit jar, though ours isn't well sealed because it's always being opened . . . They can be sandwiched or dipped in chocolate to make them fancier, though we like them just as they are in the shape of a cow. These remind me so much of my childhood, when Mum would try everything in her power to get us to sleep on time, and malty Ovaltine always seemed to be her first tactic. It didn't work, but we never let on.

150g unsalted butter, softened

100g soft light brown sugar

1 teaspoon vanilla bean paste

1 medium egg, plus 1 egg yolk

250g plain flour, sifted, plus extra for dusting

20g milk powder

75g Ovaltine powder

½ teaspoon baking powder

a pinch of fine sea salt

Prep: **15 minutes, plus 2 hours 10 minutes chilling time**
Cook: **12 minutes**   ❄: **Dough can be frozen as a roll**

Using a stand mixer or handheld mixer, cream together the butter and the sugar until they are light and fluffy. This should take about 3–4 minutes.

Add the vanilla bean paste, and mix in. Now add the egg and egg yolk gradually, and mix to combine.

Finally add the flour, milk powder, Ovaltine, baking powder and salt, and bring everything together by hand until you have a dough.

Wrap the dough in clingfilm, flatten it and chill it for at least 2 hours.

Preheat the oven to 170°C/fan 150°C, and line two baking sheets with baking paper.

Roll the dough out to about a 2mm thickness between two sheets of clingfilm, cut out your cookies (using your preferred shape) and place them on the baking sheets, making sure they are evenly spaced apart.

Keep re-rolling and cutting out shapes until you run out of dough. Prick the tops of the cookies with a fork, then put the baking sheets in the fridge for 10 minutes.

Bake for 10–12 minutes until the cookies are golden. Swap the trays around halfway through the baking time to make sure all the cookies cook evenly.

Leave the cookies to cool on the baking sheets for 10 minutes, then leave to cool completely on a wire rack.

Who stole the biscuits from the biscuit jar?

Rose Viennese swirls

Makes 12 sandwiched biscuits

These biscuits are a classic: melt-in-the-mouth with a buttery flavour. They are so delicate they should come with a 'Fragile' warning, and they are as much fun to make as they are to eat. In short, they are a little bit special, and an amazing way to show off your biscuit-making skill. Delicately sandwiched with a rose buttercream, they are also stunning to look at.

For the biscuits

250g unsalted butter, softened

100g icing sugar, sifted

250g plain flour, sifted

30g cornflour, sifted

½ teaspoon baking powder

a pinch of fine sea salt

icing sugar, for dusting

For the rose buttercream

75g unsalted butter, softened

1½ teaspoons rose syrup

175g icing sugar, sifted

Prep: **30 minutes, plus 20 minutes chilling time**
Cook: **12 minutes** ❄: **Cannot be frozen**

To make the biscuits: Line two baking sheets with baking paper or silicone pads.

Using a stand mixer or handheld mixer, cream together the butter and the sugar until they are light and fluffy. This should take about 3–4 minutes.

Now add the flour, cornflour, baking powder and salt and bring the dough together using a wooden spoon.

Put the dough in the fridge for 10 minutes.

Spoon the chilled dough into a piping bag fitted with a large star-shaped nozzle.

Pipe tight rosettes about 5cm in diameter on to the prepared baking sheets, leaving space between them, as they will spread.

Put the baking sheets in the fridge for 20 minutes to chill. Preheat the oven to 170°C/fan 150°C.

Bake the swirls on the middle shelf of the oven, one baking sheet at a time, for 10–12 minutes.

Cool on the baking sheet for 5 minutes, then leave to cool completely on a wire rack.

To make the rose buttercream: Put all the ingredients in a bowl and whisk with a handheld mixer for 3 minutes.

Put the buttercream in a piping bag fitted with a round tip. To assemble the swirls, pipe some filling on one half of a swirl, and top with another.

Lightly dust the finished swirls with icing sugar.

Salted mocha macarons

Makes 30

In all fairness, these macarons never really make it to the biscuit jar. Not only because I find myself picking sneaky hands off them, like a deranged goalie, constantly repeating 'they are not ready yet', but also, macarons always taste better the day after making, straight out of the fridge. These salted mocha macarons are delicious and easy, so do have a go. The tough part is waiting overnight to eat them at their best.

For the macarons

175g icing sugar

175g ground almonds

150g egg whites (from about 4 eggs – be sure to measure out exactly 150g)

a pinch of fine sea salt

200g caster sugar

¼ teaspoon brown gel food colouring

1 teaspoon rock salt

For the filling

100g dark chocolate (70% cocoa solids)

2 egg yolks

50g soft light brown sugar

3 tablespoons water

1½ teaspoons fine instant espresso powder

150g unsalted butter, softened

½ teaspoon rock salt

Prep: **30 minutes, plus 30 minutes resting time**
Cook: **30 minutes** ❄: **Cannot be frozen**

To make the macarons: Get two sheets of baking paper the same size as your baking sheets, and draw 30 circles on each using a 4cm cookie cutter as your guide, spaced about 1cm apart and arranged in neat lines. Turn the paper over so you don't mark the macarons, but you should still be able to see the circles.

Get a large piping bag – disposables work really well. Fit the bag with a 1cm straight-edge piping tip and place the bag in a jug, making sure to take the edge of the bag over the rim. Keeping this ready means you can work fast when the mixture for the macarons is made.

Put the icing sugar and ground almonds in the food processor and blitz for 1 minute. Add 70g of the egg whites and blitz again until it all comes together into a smooth paste.

Put the remaining egg white in a heatproof bowl with a pinch of salt, then add the caster sugar. Set the bowl over a pan of simmering water, making sure the bottom of the bowl does not touch the top of the hot water.

Beat with a handheld mixer for 4 minutes, until all the sugar has dissolved. You can check this by making sure there are no grains between your fingers when you touch the mixture.

The mixture should be thick and glossy and at the ribbon stage, which means that when the beaters are lifted they should leave a trail that stays visible for at least 3 seconds.

Now quickly put the mixture into the bowl of a stand mixer and add the food colouring. Mix for 3–4 minutes, until cooled and at the firm ribbon stage. (When you lift the beaters and leave a trail, it should stay visible for 8 seconds.) This is when it is ready.

Get the almond mixture from the food processor and put it in a bowl. Add a quarter of the meringue mixture and fold through with a large metal spoon. This should loosen the almond mixture.

Add this mixture back into the meringue mixture and, using large strokes, fold it all in until it is incorporated.

The mixture should hold a ribbon for 5 seconds and resemble thick molten lava when dropped from the spoon.

Quickly scoop the mixture into the piping bag and pipe to fill the circles you made earlier. Sprinkle each one with some rock salt.

Take the baking sheets and tap them on the edge of the work surface; this will pop any air bubbles. Set aside for 30 minutes, or until a skin has formed on top of the macarons; none of the mixture should come away on your finger. Now you can get on with the filling

Preheat the oven to 170°C/fan 150°C (do not use the fan setting if possible).

Bake the macarons one baking sheet at a time on the middle shelf for 12–13 minutes, until they are well risen and have obvious 'feet'.

Once cooked, leave them to cool on the tray.

To make the filling: Melt the chocolate in the microwave or over a pan of barely simmering water, and leave to cool.

Place the egg yolks in a heatproof bowl, and set aside.

Put the sugar, water and espresso powder in a small pan, and heat gently until the sugar has dissolved.

Now add this to the egg yolks, whisking all the time. Set the mixture over a pan of simmering water and continue to whisk gently until the mixture thickens; this should take about 3 minutes.

Take the mixture off the heat and continue to whisk.

Now gradually add the butter, and keep whisking. Fold in the melted chocolate and salt, then set the mixture aside to firm up, ready for piping. Don't refrigerate, as this will make it too hard.

To assemble the macarons, pipe some filling on one half of a macaron, and top with another.

Leave the finished macarons in the fridge overnight in an airtight container.

Spiced biscotti with an orange syllabub dip

Makes 30

These crunchy, crisp biscuits are sturdy and keep for a long time, which also makes them amazing for dunking. The fruit in the recipe can substituted with any dried fruit you may have at home. These make a great present and look really good in a jar. The syllabub is just a fancier way of serving them if you have guests around, or if you just want a treat.

For the biscotti

350g plain flour, plus extra for dusting

2 teaspoons baking powder

2 teaspoons mixed spice

250g golden caster sugar

zest of 1 orange

85g currants

85g dried cranberries

50g macadamia nuts, roughly chopped

50g pistachios, roughly chopped

3 large eggs, beaten

For the syllabub dip

300ml whipping cream

50g caster sugar

zest of 2 oranges

juice of ½ an orange

4 tablespoons whole milk

Prep: 20 minutes   Cook: 40 minutes, plus 30 minutes
❄: **Cannot be frozen**

To make the biscotti: Preheat the oven to 180°C/fan 160°C, and line two baking sheets with greaseproof paper or silicone pads.

Put the flour, baking powder, mixed spice and sugar into a bowl, and mix.

Now add the orange zest, currants, cranberries, macadamia nuts and pistachios and give everything a quick mix. Add the beaten eggs and bring the dough together by hand.

Turn the dough out on to a floured surface and divide it into two equal pieces. Roll them out to about 10cm wide and put each on a baking sheet.

Bake for 35–40 minutes, until the dough has risen and is firm, though it should still look very pale.

Take out of the oven and leave on the baking sheets. Turn the oven down to 140°C/fan 120°C.

Using a bread knife, cut diagonal slices about 1cm wide. Lay the slices out on the baking sheets, and bake for a further 25–30 minutes until dry and golden. This may take longer – just keep testing until the biscuits are very dry.

Leave the biscotti to cool on a wire rack.

To make the syllabub dip: Whisk the cream and sugar until you have soft peaks.

Add the orange zest and juice, and mix through. Add the milk to slacken the mixture so it has the consistency of a dip.

Serve in a dipping bowl alongside the biscotti.

Teatime

Depending what day of the week it is, 'tea' encompasses a very broad spectrum. A weekday usually involves us working all hours, and this equates to a hurried, no-fuss tea. Prerequisites are that it is quick, stress free, precooked . . . or made by Mum and kindly delivered by my brother, often in exchange for some raspberry jam puddle brownies. Everything is scheduled, timed and precise. Kids in, homework done, extra classes finished, dinner eaten, TV, bathtime, story and bed! Meanwhile, weekends are at the opposite end of the spectrum. They are more relaxed, and so are the prerequisites – in that there aren't any! We wake whenever it suits us. We avoid wearing proper clothes and stay in our pyjamas for as long as we can. We spend an unsavoury amount of time watching re-runs of *SpongeBob SquarePants*, and cook and eat what we want when we want it. My mum thinks that if you don't eat rice and curry for lunch and dinner, you haven't eaten properly. But since having my own children I've found my own way, with teatime meals that vary, moving from one cuisine to another, with a little bit of whatever we have to hand.

Bengali korma

Serves 4

When I hear the word 'korma', I think of the korma that has been altered by curry houses like so many Asian dishes – for the Western palate: a boneless chicken curry finished with cream. I tasted a tiny mouthful of this once out of curiosity and, while it wasn't unpleasant, I couldn't understand why they didn't stick to the original. The korma I grew up with had an aroma that took over the house and hit you in the face when you walked into the kitchen. It is the type of curry we introduce to children when they are very young – it is the mildest of curries, but also one of the tastiest by far. It is cooked with meat on the bone, in a rich sauce and finished with boiled eggs. It is one of the recipes that says 'home' to me, because nobody cooks this dish like Mum does.

5 tablespoons butter

3 tablespoons vegetable oil

1 large cinnamon stick

3 bay leaves

5 whole cardamom pods

1 whole star anise

10 cloves of garlic, peeled

7.5cm piece of ginger, peeled

2 teaspoons fine sea salt

2 large onions, finely chopped

200ml water

4 chicken thighs and 4 chicken drumsticks

6 green chillies, split lengthways and seeds removed for less heat

8 hard-boiled eggs, peeled and quartered

Prep: **20 minutes** Cook: **1 hour 30 minutes**

❄: **Can be frozen without eggs**

Put a large pan over a medium heat, and add the butter and oil. Once the oil is hot, put in the cinnamon stick, bay leaves, cardamom pods and star anise. Heat until the spices darken slightly.

Blitz the garlic and ginger in a food processor, and add a little water so that they form a paste, then add this to the pan with the salt. Cook gently over a low heat for 10 minutes.

Now add the onions and cook gently for another 20 minutes. Add the 200ml water and continue to cook gently until the onions melt down completely. To help the process along you can use a potato masher.

Be sure to keep stirring and making sure the bottom doesn't catch. What you don't want to do is colour the onions. Add water 100ml at a time if it starts to catch.

Now add the chicken to the pan, cover and leave it to cook over a medium heat, which should take around 15 minutes. Once the chicken is cooked, add the eggs and cook for 10 minutes more. Finally, add the split green chillies.

This is best served with hot basmati rice.

Cod and clementine

Serves 2

This is one of the earliest memories I have of being absolutely astonished by flavour. My mum would normally cook this dish with whole pieces of fish, and sliced fish. None of this 'easy fish', as my dad likes to call it – it was always cooked with all the bones still in, to boost the flavour. We would spend a long time picking it apart to eat it, and placing the bones a safe distance away from our plates. Traditionally we'd eat it with our hands (it's near enough impossible with cutlery). Although it was delicious, these days there isn't always time to sit at our plates for an hour, and since having my own kids I am the biggest fan of filleted fish. Granted, it imparts less flavour to this dish – but the clementine peel well and truly makes up for that.

5 tablespoons olive oil

2 cloves of garlic, crushed

½ onion, diced

1 tablespoon tomato purée

1 teaspoon fine sea salt

200ml water

½ teaspoon turmeric

1 teaspoon paprika

1 teaspoon ground cumin

2 clementines, peel only, sliced

juice of 1 clementine

300g cod fillets

a large handful of coriander, finely chopped

Prep: **15 minutes**   Cook: **40 minutes**   ❄: **Cannot be frozen**

Heat the oil in a medium pan over a medium heat. Once hot, add the crushed garlic and diced onion. Turn the heat down and cook gently until the onions are soft.

Add the tomato purée, salt and water. Cook for a further 5 minutes over a low heat.

Now add the turmeric, paprika and cumin, and cook gently for another 5 minutes. Keep adding small amounts of water if it starts to catch on the bottom.

Add the clementine peel and cook for 10 minutes, until the peel is soft and almost falling apart.

Use a potato masher to mash all the peel – breaking it up will intensify the flavour.

Add the fish, cover and cook for 10 minutes over a low heat. Squeeze in the clementine juice. Once the fish is cooked, take the pan off the heat and sprinkle over the chopped coriander.

This dish is best eaten with hot basmati rice.

Dill, fennel and mussel linguine

Serves 2

I know mussels can be daunting and if you have never ventured into cooking them before, give this a go. Just make sure you get the best mussels which are as fresh as possible. I absolutely adore the flavours of the sea, especially when they're paired with herbs, and I have to say mussels and dill seem to work so well together. This dish is light, but subtly flavoured with herbs and fragrant fennel. It's a delicious way of eating mussels with the added substance of the linguine. Served hot with a squeeze of lemon juice, this is light, tasty and easy.

2 tablespoons vegetable oil

3 cloves of garlic, crushed

½ fennel bulb, very thinly sliced

½ teaspoon fine sea salt

½ teaspoon dried chilli flakes

1 anchovy fillet

250g linguine

1kg mussels, cleaned

a small bunch of fresh dill, chopped

freshly ground black pepper

a squeeze of lemon juice

olive oil, for drizzling

Prep: **20 minutes**   Cook: **15 minutes**   ❄: **Cannot be frozen**

Bring a large pan of salted water to the boil.

Put another large pan over a low heat and add the oil, then add the garlic and cook for 1 minute. Next add the fennel, salt, chilli flakes and anchovy. Cook for a few more minutes, until everything is soft.

Put the linguine in the pan of boiling water, and cook following the packet instructions.

Put the mussels on top of the fennel mixture, cover and cook until all the mussels have opened. If any remain closed, throw them away.

Drain the cooked pasta, reserving a little cooking liquid.

Add the pasta to the cooked mussels, along with the reserved liquid. Sprinkle over the dill, some pepper, and squirt with lemon juice.

Serve in bowls, drizzled with olive oil.

Dry tomato tiger prawns with pooris

Serves 2

Prawns just make me giddy with excitement. Not the precooked, prepacked pink variety, but the raw kind. I love spending time taking the shells off and de-veining them over the sink as I watch the kids play in the garden. In this dish you cook the base first for a long time, to get the most flavour from the sweet tomatoes and garlic. Then you cook the prawns for a few minutes only, being careful not to overcook them. Partnered with the crisp, buttery poori pastries, they are best eaten by hand – the messier, the better.

For the prawns

5 tablespoons olive oil

5 cloves of garlic, finely chopped

1 small onion, finely chopped

1 green chilli, finely chopped

1 tablespoon tomato purée

2 medium tomatoes, finely chopped

½ teaspoon turmeric

½ teaspoon paprika

1 teaspoon ground cumin

300g raw tiger prawns, shelled and de-veined

a handful of coriander, finely chopped

For the pooris

35g plain flour, plus extra for dusting

½ teaspoon fine sea salt

10g unsalted butter, melted

200ml cold water

1 litre vegetable oil, for frying

Prep: 25 minutes   Cook: 25 minutes   ❄: Cannot be frozen

To make the prawns: Put the oil in a medium pan over a medium heat, add the garlic and brown it gently, making sure it doesn't burn. Add the onion and green chilli and cook gently for 5 minutes, until the onions have softened (if the onion sticks, add a tablespoon or two of water).

Add the tomato purée and chopped tomatoes, and cook over a low heat for 10 minutes, uncovered, until they have softened and formed a smooth paste. Now add the spices, and cook gently for another 5 minutes. By now the tomatoes will be very dry. Finally, add the cleaned prawns and cook until they are just pink. Take the pan off the heat, and mix the coriander through.

To make the pooris: Put the flour, salt and melted butter into a large bowl. Slowly add the water, and bring the mixture together until you have a firm, dry dough (you may need a little more or less water). Knead for 2 minutes on a lightly floured surface.

Heat the oil in a large frying pan over a high heat for a few minutes and then turn the heat down. Divide the poori dough into golf-ball-sized pieces. Take each ball and roll it out on a floured surface. The pooris should be the size of a grapefruit and 3mm thick.

Gently slide the pooris into the oil in the pan using a slotted spoon and allow to puff up. This should take about 1 minute. Turn them over and cook the other side for 1 minute. They should be golden and fluffy. Drain them on kitchen paper, while you cook the rest. Leave the cooked pooris uncovered, or they will go soggy.

To serve, spoon a generous amount of the prawns into the centre of each poori, leaving room on the outer edge for you to tear and dip into the centre.

Quick and easy boiled egg curry

Serves 4–6

This was a curry that Mum often cooked when we didn't have a lot to eat. When I say 'not a lot to eat', this probably meant 'three curries left' but Mum wanted something extra. We always had a minimum of four curries on the table – only when she was too busy to cook six. I always wondered how she did it. It's safe to say I haven't entirely adopted her attitude to feeding the family. Even though as a housewife I have dedicated a lot of time to cooking, I only ever cook one curry, to serve with rice: we try to enjoy a good meal without quite so much gluttony. This is a great recipe for when you want a delicious curry fast, and I have even been known to put it in the kids' sandwiches the following day. Simply smother each piece of bread with the thick curry paste and slice some eggs into it, and that's your alternative egg sandwich done.

5 tablespoons vegetable oil

2 bay leaves

2 medium onions, peeled and finely chopped

2 tomatoes, finely chopped

2 green chillies, split

1 teaspoon fine sea salt

1 teaspoon turmeric

2 teaspoons ground cumin

2 teaspoons paprika

200ml water

6 hardboiled eggs, peeled and lightly scored all over

3 tablespoons vegetable oil

a large bunch of coriander, chopped

Prep: 10 minutes   Cook: **25 minutes**   ❄: **Cannot be frozen**

Put a large wok over a medium heat. Add 5 tablespoons of the oil and the bay leaves, and heat until they are golden, then add the onions, tomatoes, chillies and salt.

Cook for 10 minutes, stirring occasionally, until everything has softened and the onions and tomatoes have broken down.

Now add all the spices and the water, and simmer for 15 minutes until the contents of the pan have reduced to a thick dry paste.

Heat the remaining 3 tablespoons oil in a frying pan, then add the eggs. Fry them to create a crisp shell around the outside of the eggs.

Now add the fried, hardboiled eggs to the tomato and onion base. Frying the eggs allows this paste to stick to the outside of the egg.

Add the coriander, give everything a good stir and serve the curry with rice, flatbreads or even poppadoms. We even like to mix it with pasta – everyone gets one of the eggs to break up and mix through.

Green mango and fish curry

Serves 2–3

I was raised in a family in which fish was cooked every single day. Where we are from in Bangladesh, fish is readily available and eaten in abundance, and very often is combined with fruit. So whenever my mum managed to source green mango, she would make this wonderful curry. As children we were always astonished by how vibrant it looked, and this is still a talking point among the newest generation of our family. It has a subtle hint of garlic, and the tartness from the unripe mango is simply delicious. It is a light and fresh curry that goes perfectly with rice.

3 tablespoons olive oil

5 cloves of garlic, chopped

1 teaspoon ground turmeric

½ teaspoon chilli powder

2 small green (unripe) mangoes, peeled, stoned and sliced

½ teaspoon fine sea salt

1 teaspoon tamarind paste

200ml water

400g haddock fillets, skinned, cut into chunks

3 green chillies, split lengthways

a large handful of coriander, finely chopped

Prep: **20 minutes**   Cook: **25 minutes**   ❄: **Cannot be frozen**

Put a medium pan over a medium heat, and add the oil and the garlic. Cook until the garlic is golden, then add the turmeric, chilli powder, green mangoes and salt, and cook over a low heat for 3 minutes.

Now add the tamarind paste and the water, and lower the heat. Leave everything to cook for 10 minutes, until the mango is tender but has not completely melted away.

Add the fish and stir it in. Cover and cook for a further 10 minutes.

Once the fish is cooked, take the pan off the heat and add the sliced chillies and coriander.

Serve with hot basmati rice.

Lemon thyme Irish stew

Serves 4

At the age of twelve, my baby brother suddenly became a bit more interested in eating, and eventually cooking. Even though my parents cook every day, he never took a massive interest in their traditional cooking, and was more into other cuisines. I was always tinkering away with new recipes and ideas, and so he joined me on that journey, and has kind of been with me on it ever since. This was the first proper thing he cooked under my watchful eye, and it is still a firm favourite when he comes round. It is a traditional meat and veg stew, but the added aroma of lemon thyme, zest and fresh herbs elevates the whole thing. With crusty bread to mop up the juices, it is one of our favourites.

1kg diced mutton

4 tablespoons plain flour

4 tablespoons vegetable oil

12 baby carrots, scrubbed (or 3 medium carrots, chopped into 1cm pieces)

12 baby onions, unpeeled

400ml chicken stock

12 baby potatoes, scrubbed

a large sprig of lemon thyme

a large handful of fresh parsley, chopped

a large handful of fresh chives, chopped

zest of 1 lemon

salt and freshly ground black pepper

Prep: 20 minutes | **Cook: 2 hours 30 minutes** | ❄: Can be frozen

Preheat the oven to 160°C/fan 140°C.

Toss the meat in the flour, making sure it is lightly coated. This will help to thicken the sauce. Put a large pan over a medium heat. Add the oil then add the meat in batches, making sure not to overcrowd the pan. Brown the meat and then set aside in a bowl.

Now add the carrots and onions to the same pan, and cook for 5 minutes. Season generously with salt and pepper, then add the meat back to the pan along with the stock. Bring to the boil and then pop in the potatoes.

Finally, add the thyme sprig and transfer everything to an ovenproof casserole. Cook in the oven for 2 hours.

Add the chopped fresh herbs and lemon zest, give everything a good stir to combine, and serve. Don't forget to remove the thyme stalks, though.

Manchego and chorizo calzone

Serves 8

I love making what my kids call an 'inside-out pizza'. In fact I didn't discover calzone until a pizza delivery went wrong and we got one by accident. Rather than argue over a refund with a very grumpy tummy and even grumpier husband in the background – I decided to keep it and just fill the hole. It turned out I was mesmerised by the crisp, crunchy shell hiding a moist and tender filling, and have been perfecting my own version ever since. There are so many ways of getting the dough to crisp up involving baking stones, but I prefer to use what I have to hand. I simply heat a baking sheet in a very hot oven before sprinkling over some semolina, ready to bake the calzone.

For the dough

500g strong bread flour, plus extra for dusting

1 teaspoon fine sea salt

1 teaspoon sugar

7g fast-action yeast

1 tablespoon vegetable oil, plus extra for greasing

320ml water

2 tablespoons semolina

For the filling

8 cherry tomatoes, halved

50g chorizo sausage, cubed (or veggie sausage or paneer)

1 large red chilli, sliced

5 anchovy fillets, chopped

50g manchego cheese, thinly sliced

salt and freshly ground black pepper, to taste

20g salted butter, melted

Prep: **25 minutes**   Cook: **15 minutes**
❄: Can't be frozen before baking

Put the bread flour in the bowl of a stand mixer, then add the salt to one side and the sugar and yeast on the other. Make a well in the middle, and add the oil. Give everything a quick mix, then start adding the water slowly until the dough comes together. You may not need all the water.

Mix the dough on medium for 6 minutes, until it is smooth and elastic.

Grease a large bowl and tip the dough into it. Cover and leave for 1 hour, or until the dough has doubled in size. Knock all the air out of the dough, then spilt it into two equal pieces.

Preheat the oven to gas 240°C/fan 220°C, and put two baking sheets in there to heat up.

On a floured surface, roll out the two pieces of dough to 35 x 25cm rectangles.

Start putting the filling ingredients lengthways down the centre of the two rectangles. Season with salt and pepper to taste. Fold over one long edge of each calzone to meet the other, and crimp them together.

Take the hot baking sheets out of the oven, and sprinkle them with semolina. Put the two calzones on the baking sheets, and bake for 15 minutes, when the dough will be golden all over.

Once the calzones are cooked, brush the tops with melted butter and sprinkle with a little salt, then serve with a rocket salad.

Mustard kale mac and cheese

Serves 6

I am not averse to a massive bowl of mac and cheese for dinner, but it took a while to convince my family that sometimes this is OK: it doesn't always have to be rice and curry, or curry and rice. I don't mean the kind that comes out of a can and isn't sure if it is mac and cheese or baby custard mixed with overcooked pasta – it doesn't have to be like a school dinner nightmare. Proper home-cooked mac and cheese is warm, hearty and delicious. This recipe, with mustard and kale to add interest, makes for a delicious one-pot meal.

500g pasta

1 tablespoon vegetable oil

2 tablespoons unsalted butter

3 cloves of garlic, crushed

1 teaspoon English mustard powder

3 tablespoons plain flour

250ml whole milk

250ml single cream

250g mature Cheddar cheese, grated

a large handful of kale leaves, chopped

50g Parmesan cheese, grated

freshly ground black pepper

Prep: 15 minutes   Cook: **25 minutes**   ❄: **Can be frozen**

Preheat the oven to 200°C/fan 180°C.

Bring a large pan of salted water to the boil, and cook the pasta for 3 minutes less than the recommended time on the packet. Drain and add the oil, stirring it through. This will stop the pasta sticking together.

Melt the butter in a small pan over a medium heat, then add the garlic and mustard powder and cook for 1 minute.

Stir in the flour, and cook for another minute, mixing all the time.

Add the milk and the cream, and whisk until the sauce is smooth and lump-free. Continue to whisk until the sauce thickens.

Take the pan off the heat, add the grated Cheddar cheese and leave it to melt, stirring occasionally.

Now tip the pasta and kale into an ovenproof dish, and pour over the sauce. Bake for 20 minutes, until the top is crisp and golden.

Sprinkle with the Parmesan and a good grind of black pepper to serve.

Pink peppered steak with sweet potato wedges

Serves 2

My family are great meat-eaters. The thought of not eating meat would send a shudder down the spines of generations past, present and future. (Mind you, about sixteen years ago I decided that I loved animals so much I never wanted to eat one again. I lasted a monumental twelve hours.) Every year for a particular religious festival my dad orders an entire sheep, butchered and delivered to our door. Before the meat is handed out, Dad gives the order: 'Let's see how much steak you can eat.' He is always astonished at how much we get through as he calculates the cost of our meat-eating frenzy. Anyway, these peppered steaks are fragrant, aromatic and spicy; I like to bash the meat to make it thinner, but you can leave yours thicker if you want. Cook the steaks to your liking and pair with sweet potato wedges for a hearty dinner that even my dad would approve of . . . despite how much it costs him.

For the steak

2 heaped teaspoons pink peppercorns

1 small red onion, roughly chopped

2 tablespoons olive oil

60g salted butter

fine sea salt, to taste

2 large steaks (beef, lamb or mutton), bashed with a rolling pin between two sheets of clingfilm to make them really thin

double cream (optional)

For the sweet potato wedges

2 medium sweet potatoes, skin on, washed and cut into wedges

4 tablespoons olive oil

1 tablespoon garlic powder

1 teaspoon paprika

salt and freshly ground black pepper, to taste

Prep: 10 minutes   **Cook: 2 minutes**   ❄: **Cannot be frozen**

To cook the steak: Put the pink peppercorns, red onion, oil and butter in a food processor, and blitz for a few seconds until roughly chopped. Set aside.

Heat a large non-stick pan over a high heat. Season the steaks with salt, then put the peppercorn mixture into the pan and cook for 2 minutes. Take the onion and peppercorn paste out and put in a bowl. Put the seasoned steaks into the pan, and cook for 3 minutes on each side, or to your liking.

Once the steaks are cooked, set them aside on a plate covered with foil to rest for 10 minutes.

Serve the rested steaks with the sauce on top. Add a few table-spoons of double cream to the sauce and heat gently just before serving for an especially decadent addition.

To make the wedges: Preheat the oven to 200°C/fan 180°C.

Toss the wedges in a bowl with the olive oil, garlic powder, paprika, salt and pepper.

Put them into a large roasting tin and bake for 15–20 minutes, until light brown. Serve alongside the steak.

Softened sweet onion and crisp fried fish

Serves 3

This was a recipe that only ever really got made when guests were coming round – it's a staple in the array of dishes usually made for such a banquet. However, it is great simply eaten with boiled white rice or a salad. It can be cooked with whole small fish, slices of fish, or even fillets. The fish is marinated in spices and fried at a high temperature to give it a crisp skin. Left to cool, it is then served on top of the sweet sautéed onions.

3 tilapia fillets, sliced lengthways (alternatively, you could use cod, haddock or any white fish fillets)

oil, for frying

½ teaspoon turmeric

1 teaspoon paprika

½ teaspoon ground cumin

½ teaspoon ground coriander

1 teaspoon fine sea salt

1 teaspoon freshly ground black pepper

1 teaspoon mustard seeds

2 medium onions, sliced

3 chillies, split lengthways and deseeded

½ teaspoon salt

a large handful of coriander, finely chopped

Prep: 15 minutes   **Cook: 15 minutes**   ❄: **Cannot be frozen**

Pat the fish dry as much as possible with kitchen paper – this will stop the fish spitting when you fry it. Put the fish in a bowl, and add about 2 tablespoons of vegetable oil, the spices, and salt and pepper, then give everything a good mix, so all the fish is coated.

Heat 5 tablespoons of vegetable oil in a large non-stick frying pan until it is smoking hot. Now add the marinated fish, but don't be tempted to move it. Let it cook for 3 minutes on each side. Once cooked, remove the fish from the pan and place on kitchen paper.

Now add the mustard seeds to the same pan, over a medium heat. The seeds will start to pop, and at this point add the onions and chillies. Cook gently until the onions are soft, then add the salt and the coriander.

Spread the onions out on a platter, top with the fried fish and serve.

Spiced turkey and mushroom pie

Serves 4

When I make a roast, I often make it for the masses . . . even though there are only five of us for dinner. I always worry 'What if someone turns up and there's no food for them?' And this is why I am often found making something new out of something old. I always find the meat too dry for sandwiches by the next day, so instead I make a spiced version of a poultry and mushroom pie. This gives leftovers a new lease of life and, topped with a lid of puff pastry, it makes for delicious one-pot meal.

2 tablespoons vegetable oil

3 cloves of garlic, crushed

2.5cm piece of ginger, very finely chopped

1 medium onion, finely chopped

1 tablespoon tomato purée

1 teaspoon ground cinnamon

1 teaspoon ground cumin

1 teaspoon chilli flakes

1 teaspoon fine sea salt

300ml chicken stock

325g button mushrooms, quartered

275g leftover turkey, cut into chunks

1 sheet of puff pastry

1 medium egg, beaten

Prep: 20 minutes   Cook: 50 minutes   ❄: Cannot be frozen

Heat the oil over a medium heat in a large, deep pan, and sauté the garlic and ginger for 2 minutes, then add the onion and the tomato purée.

Now add all the spices and the salt. Cook for a few minutes until the mixture has softened. If it starts to stick, add a little bit of the stock.

Add the mushrooms and the turkey, followed by the chicken stock. Leave everything to simmer, uncovered, for 10 minutes, until some of the liquid has evaporated.

Put all of the pie filling into a large deep, oven-proof pie dish, and leave it to cool. Meanwhile, preheat the oven to 180°C/fan 160°C.

Now roll out the puff pastry to the right size, and put it on top of the dish, crimping the edges to seal them. Glaze the top with the egg, and make a hole in the centre of the pie for steam to escape. Put it on a baking sheet, and bake in the middle of the oven for 25 minutes until the pastry is golden brown and puffed up.

Dessert for dinner

One day I was in a basement, keeping an eye on the boys through a window during their martial arts class. I remember that day clearly: I just watched them and wondered how fast they were growing; I look at them again now and marvel at how fast they have actually grown. Sometimes I can't believe my eyes or my luck. I have beautiful children, and I live to make their every waking moment a happy one. But only after their homework and chores are done, of course! I do have to play the bad guy sometimes . . . but I aim to make the rest of the time great. So I had this idea that has since transformed our lives, but only once a month. You heard right – just once a month. On that day, we have dessert for dinner. It can be anything from cake to biscuits, from custard to crème brûlé, or from ice cream to whipped cream. They can have whatever they like, with no mention of anything savoury or salty – unless of course it's salted caramel. I'm still watching my once-babies grow every day, and maybe in the future I will come up with a better idea to treat them with. An idea better suited to them as they grow. But for now dessert for dinner works just fine, and I have a funny feeling that this tradition will stay with us for a while. It might even follow through to another generation. Here's hoping . . .

Blueberry and vanilla clafoutis

Serves 6

I love nothing more than a dessert that is quick and easy to make – especially the kind that can be prepared beforehand and then baked when you are ready to eat it. This clafoutis is best eaten fresh, but you can make the batter up to 24 hours in advance and refrigerate until ready to use. Serving up a pudding straight from the oven makes you look like domestic goddess, and is a surefire crowd-pleaser. The steps for putting this together are so simple, and the mixture of vanilla and blueberries is delicious. It's best served warm, but don't be too eager and scorch your mouth. I speak from experience. Leave it to cool just slightly, and serve it with pouring cream.

4 medium eggs

160g plain flour

160g unsalted butter,
  melted and cooled

300ml whole milk

120g caster sugar

1 vanilla pod, split
  lengthways, or
  1 teaspoon vanilla
  bean paste

40g unsalted butter

300g blueberries

1 tablespoon granulated
  sugar, for sprinkling

Prep: **15 minutes**   Cook: **30 minutes**   ❄: **Cannot be frozen**

Preheat the oven to 200°C/fan 180°C.

Lightly beat the eggs in a mixing bowl with a whisk, then lightly beat in the flour. Whisk in the cooled melted butter, then gradually whisk in the milk, then the sugar. Finally, whisk in the vanilla seeds (scraped from the pods) or the vanilla paste.

Use the 40g butter to generously line the inside of a baking dish, approximately 25cm in diameter and 4cm deep. Put all the blueberries in the base of the greased dish, and and pour over the batter.

Bake for 10 minutes, then lower the temperature to 180°C/fan 160°C. Bake for a further 10 minutes and check to see if the clafoutis is cooked by inserting a skewer in the centre and seeing if it comes out clean. If not, continue to bake and check at 5-minute intervals.

Remove from the oven and allow to cool for 10 minutes before serving. The clafoutis will sink very slightly as it cools; if you want to serve it before it sinks make sure you make people aware that it is very hot.

Sprinkle the top with granulated sugar before serving.

Choc chip cookie dough and macadamia ice cream

Serves 6/Makes 1 litre

I never really delved into making my own ice cream until I watched a TV programme that showed what goes into the mass-produced stuff. Did that put me off? Not really, if I'm honest. We don't eat ice cream that often, so it didn't feel awful to eat it if and when we did buy it. It was only really when I bought an ice-cream maker on sale that I started to contemplate recipes. Once I realised how easy it was to make ice cream I really gave it a go, and among the first I made was a cookie dough version. This is one of my favourite ice-cream flavours, and it tastes even better when it's homemade – you can use an indecent amount of cream and cookie dough. This makes quite a large quantity, as I like to freeze any excess for baking at a later date.

For the cookie dough

125g plain flour

½ teaspoon fine sea salt

85g unsalted butter, softened in the microwave

50g brown sugar

1 teaspoon vanilla bean paste

4 tablespoons whole milk

150g milk chocolate chips

100g macadamia nuts, roasted and roughly chopped

For the ice cream

250ml whole milk

250ml double cream

125g caster sugar

1 vanilla pod, split lengthways

6 egg yolks

Prep: 25 minutes   Cook: 15 minutes (plus cooling and freezing)
❄: **Will keep for up to 6 months in the freezer; best eaten within 1 month**

To make the cookie dough: Put the flour, salt, butter, brown sugar, vanilla bean paste, milk and chocolate chips into a bowl or a stand mixer.

Mix until the dough comes together. If it doesn't, add more milk a tablespoon at a time until it does.

Put the dough between two sheets of clingfilm, and roll it out to a thickness of 1cm, then put it in the freezer so it will be easier to cut.

To make the ice cream: Mix the milk and cream together in a saucepan. Add about 80g of the sugar to the pan, along with the vanilla pod. Slowly bring the mixture to the boil, then take off the heat and set aside.

In the meantime mix the egg yolks with the remaining sugar, and whisk with a handheld mixer until it reaches a light ribbon stage (when the beaters are lifted, a trail of the mixture is left behind).

Pour the boiled cream mixture slowly into the beaten eggs, making sure to stir all the time, then pour the mixture back into the pan.

Cook the custard over a low heat for about 10 minutes, stirring with a spatula. Do not let it boil, or it will curdle. The custard is ready when it has thickened enough to coat the back of the spatula. When you run your finger down the spatula it should leave a distinct trace.

Now run the custard through a sieve, and leave it to cool completely. Once cooled, remove the vanilla pod, then put the custard in an ice-cream maker and churn for 20 minutes, or according to the manufacturer's instructions. If you don't have an ice-cream machine, the mixture can be placed in a large (preferably shallow) Tupperware and placed in the freezer. Make sure to give it a good stir with a fork every hour and a half, as this will prevent crystallization. It can take up to 6 hours to freeze.

While the ice cream is churning, cut the cookie dough into 1cm pieces. Once the ice cream is churned or has spent around 6 hours in the freezer, mix in the cookie dough and the chopped macadamia nuts. Stir roughly and freeze again for 30 minutes before serving. Take it out of the freezer 5–10 minutes before serving so that it is soft enough to scoop.

Chocolate and hazelnut profiteroles

Serves 6/Makes about 24

My dad's all-time favourite dessert is profiteroles or éclairs – or 'eclix', as he likes to call them! Although I make them all the time and freeze them for whenever Dad might pop by, I also love making them fresh and playing with the flavours. Here I have kept the choux and the cream filling simple, but have added the flavour of roasted hazelnuts to elevate the chocolate. This a great recipe for preparing in advance and assembling just before serving.

For the choux pastry

85g unsalted butter

220ml hot water

105g plain flour

a pinch of fine sea salt

4 medium eggs

For the filling

400ml double cream

2 tablespoons icing sugar

For the hazelnut chocolate

160g dark chocolate (at least 60% cocoa solids)

2 tablespoons hazelnut syrup

50g unsalted butter

100g hazelnuts, roasted and chopped

Prep: 40 minutes   **Cook: 35 minutes**   ❄: **Can be frozen unfilled**

To make the choux pastry: Preheat the oven to 200°C/fan 180°C, and line two baking sheets with greaseproof paper or silicone pads.

Put the butter and water in a large non-stick pan over a high heat. Once the water comes to the boil, take the pan off the heat and add the flour and salt. Mix the dough fast with a wooden spoon for about 3 minutes until it becomes a smooth paste with no lumps.

Leave the pan to cool for 5 minutes, then add the eggs one by one, stirring between each. The batter will appear lumpy, but just keep mixing until it is smooth. When ready, it should be a stiff, slightly stubborn mixture that will reluctantly fall off your spoon.

Put the mixture into a piping bag and pipe walnut-sized dollops on to the lined baking sheets. Space them about 2cm apart, as they will puff up. If there are any peaks sticking up use a wet finger to tap them down, otherwise they will catch in the oven.

Bake for 20 minutes, until golden brown and crisp. Remove from the baking sheets, and pierce the base of each with the end of a teaspoon, making a decent hole for the steam to escape. This will also create a hole to pipe the cream into. Leave to cool on a wire rack.

To make the filling: Whip the cream with the icing sugar into stiff peaks, then transfer it to a piping bag and chill it in the fridge.

To make the hazelnut chocolate: Melt the chocolate in the micro-wave or over a pan of simmering water. Add the hazelnut syrup and the butter and mix with a wooden spoon until it is nice and smooth.

To assemble the profiteroles: Pipe each profiterole full of the whipped cream. They will feel heavy when they are full. Put them on a tray and drizzle with lots of the hazelnut chocolate, then sprinkle with the chopped roasted hazelnuts. Keep the profiteroles in the fridge if you're not serving them straight away.

Chocolate and star anise fondants

Serves 8

Chocolate fondants have a horrible reputation of being among the scariest desserts to bake. It took me until my late twenties to even attempt this beast. I want to tell you it went horribly wrong, that it was an inedible disaster. But I'm sorry to say it went really well, and it always has. This is a safe and easy recipe for a melt-in-the-middle sensation. Crusty on the outside, warm and gooey on the inside with the distinctive, lingering aroma of anise.

For the coating

50g unsalted butter, melted

cocoa powder, for dusting

For the fondants

200g dark chocolate (70% cocoa solids), melted

200g unsalted butter, melted

200g caster sugar

4 whole medium eggs, plus 4 egg yolks

200g plain flour, sifted

4 teaspoons star anise, ground with a pestle and mortar and passed through a small, fine sieve

Prep: **20 minutes, plus chilling**   Cook: **15 minutes**
❄: **Can be frozen before baking**

To coat the ramekins: Brush 8 ramekins with melted butter, making upward strokes. Place the ramekins on a baking tray in the freezer for 10 minutes.

Take the ramekins out again and brush them once more with melted butter, and put them back in the freezer for 10 minutes. Take them out and dust the insides with cocoa powder, making sure to tap out any excess.

To make the fondants: Preheat the oven to 200°C/fan 180°C.

Melt the chocolate in a bowl over a pan of simmering water, being careful not to allow the bowl to touch the water. Roughly chop the butter and add to the chocolate, stirring until it melts in.

Whisk the sugar and eggs until they are light and fluffy and doubled in size. This will take about 5 minutes in a stand mixer, or 5–10 minutes with a handheld mixer. Add the butter and chocolate mixture, and mix everything together. Now add the flour and star anise, and fold in using a large metal spoon.

Put the ramekins on a baking tray. Divide the mixture between the ramekins, leaving a 1cm gap at the top of each. Cook for 10–12 minutes, no longer. The fondants will start to come away from the sides of the ramekins.

Take the fondants out of the oven, and leave in the ramekins for 1 minute only. They will still be hot, but they need to be turned out straight away and served, otherwise the residual heat will cook them right through.

You can freeze the fondants before baking, ready for another occasion. If you are cooking from frozen, cook at 200°C/fan 180°C for 17 minutes.

Coconut, pineapple and fennel cream pie

Serves 8

Here the crisp buttery base of the pie, with the fennel and coconut custard, topped with cold whipped cream and toasted coconut, is just divine. This is my mum's signature flavour combination (among the few sweet things she makes) and I love using it in as many desserts as possible; she always beams with pride when I find another way. So this is another one for Mum . . . but I had to add the pineapple for an extra dimension – tartness and texture.

For the pastry

225g plain flour, plus extra for dusting

110g unsalted butter, chilled and diced

80g caster sugar

1 large egg

For the filling

240ml coconut cream

350ml double cream

4 large egg yolks

140g caster sugar

35g cornflour

½ teaspoon fine sea salt

2 teaspoons fennel seeds, toasted and crushed

200g fresh pineapple, cored and thinly sliced

For the topping

350ml double cream

2 tablespoons icing sugar

3 tablespoons coconut flakes, toasted

Prep: 40 minutes, plus chilling   Cook: 45 minutes

To make the pastry: Put the flour, butter and caster sugar in a food processor, and blitz to the consistency of breadcrumbs, or this can be done by hand. Add the egg and blitz again; the dough should come together. Wrap in clingfilm and chill for 30 minutes.

On a floured surface, roll out the pastry as thinly as you can (ideally the thickness of a pound coin), making sure it's big enough to line the base and sides of your tart tin (23cm diameter).

Line the tart tin, leaving the pastry overhanging around the edge, and put it on a baking sheet. Prick the base of the tart shell all over with a fork. Put the pastry case in the fridge to chill for 30 minutes.

Preheat the oven to 200°C/fan 180°C. Cover the tart shell with greaseproof paper, and fill with baking beads; this will stop the pastry from rising during baking. Bake for 13 minutes, then remove the greaseproof paper and beads. Bake for a further 13 minutes. The tart shell should be golden and crisp. If the pastry is still a little undercooked in the corners, return to the oven and check at 3-minute intervals. If the pastry is becoming too dark on the edges, cover lightly with foil. Set it aside to cool.

Trim off any excess pastry with a small, serrated knife. Remove the pastry tart from the tin and put on a wire rack to cool completely.

To make the filling: Slowly bring the coconut cream and the double cream to the boil in a small pan, then take off the heat.

In a bowl, whisk the egg yolks, caster sugar, cornflour and salt for a few minutes.

Slowly add the hot cream mixture to the whisked egg and sugar mixture, stirring all the time with a wooden spoon. Now put all the mixture back into the pan, add the crushed fennel seeds, and continue to stir gently over a medium heat until it thickens. This should take about 10 minutes. The mixture needs to be very thick. If it gets too hot, however, the fat from the coconut cream will start to separate. If this happens, remove from the heat and quickly whisk in 1 teaspoon sieved icing sugar or 2 teaspoons cold water, and it should come back together.

Pour the hot filling into the tart shell. Leave to cool at room temperature, then cover with a large bowl or loosely with foil and leave to cool further in the fridge for 1 hour.

Once completely cooled, lay the sliced pineapple on top.

To make the topping: Whip the cream and the icing sugar to soft peaks. Cover the top of the pie with the cream and sprinkle with the toasted coconut flakes

Mango and parsley pavlova

Serves 8

My freezer is the world hub of egg whites. I never throw them away when I am baking, and unless I am planning to use them straight away I freeze them in batches of five for when I am making a pavlova. I also love sweet mangoes – they're a sure sign that summer is looming, but these days you can buy rich, sweet mangoes tinned in syrup all year round. They are quite delicious on their own, but mixed with parsley and a hint of lime they pair with the meringue to make a stunning dessert.

For the meringue

1 teaspoon white vinegar

1 teaspoon vanilla extract

5 egg whites

a pinch of fine sea salt

250g caster sugar

1 teaspoon cream
  of tartar

3 teaspoons cornflour

For the cream

160ml whipping cream

4 tablespoons icing sugar

350g plain yoghurt

For the fruit topping

2 large ripe Alphonso
  mangoes, peeled,
  stoned and chopped
  into chunks

zest of 2 limes and juice
  of 1 lime

a handful of parsley,
  chopped (⅓ small pack)

50g flaked almonds,
  toasted

Prep: **25 minutes**   Cook: **1 hour, plus cooling**   ❄: **Cannot be frozen**

To make the meringue: Cut a sheet of baking paper to fit a baking sheet, and draw a circle in the centre, about 24cm in diameter. Turn the paper over so you don't get ink on your meringue, and line the baking sheet. Preheat the oven to 140°C/fan 120°C.

Put the vinegar and vanilla extract in a large, clean bowl. Now add the egg whites, and whisk with a handheld mixer until the eggs reach soft peaks. Add the salt, then slowly add the sugar, continuing to whisk.

The egg white will start to get shiny. Once the sugar is all added, mix in the cream of tartar and the cornflour. The meringue should now be really stiff.

Spoon the meringue mixture on to the circle on the lined baking sheet, making sure to create a slight dip the centre to hold the cream and the fruit.

Bake for 1 hour, then turn the oven off and leave the meringue inside until the oven is completely cold. (Baked meringue will keep in an airtight tin for up to 5 days.)

To make the cream: Whip the cream with the icing sugar until you have stiff peaks. Add the yoghurt, and mix it through well.

Top the pavlova with the cream.

To make the fruit topping: Put the chunks of mango, the lime zest and juice and the chopped parsley in a bowl, and mix together.

Spoon the fruit mixture on top of the cream and sprinkle the finished pavlova with the toasted almonds.

Mint dark chocolate and raspberry mousse pots

Serves 2

This recipe could not be any simpler, but it's unusual in that it uses water – usually kept apart from chocolate. It is rich and dense, so a little bit goes a very long way. It can be adapted with sprinkles and cookies to make it perfect for a kids' party, but I love the bitter sweetness of the chocolate with mint and the freshness of raspberries. This is a go-to recipe for all your pregnant guests, as there are no raw eggs in it, and it's perfect for vegans, too. It will keep for 2–3 days in the fridge.

125g dark chocolate (60% cocoa solids), broken into chunks

125ml boiled water

10 mint leaves, chopped, plus extra sprigs to decorate

4 raspberries

1 tablespoon cocoa powder, for dusting

Prep: **10 minutes, plus cooling**   Cook: **10 minutes**
❅: **Cannot be frozen**

Melt the chocolate in the microwave or over a pan of simmering water.

Add the boiled water to the melted chocolate, mixing continuously with a wooden spoon. Keep mixing as it cools and thickens. Now add the chopped mint, and mix it through.

Put a fresh raspberry in the bottom of each pot (or use espresso cups). Pour the chocolate mixture into a jug, then pour it into the pots.

Put the pots on a baking sheet, and leave them to set in the fridge for 1 hour.

Top each pot with a raspberry and a sprig of mint, then dust with cocoa powder.

Nutmeg and orange baked cheesecake

Serves 10

A baked cheesecake is a labour of love; there are a few stages, and a lot of leaving it around in the oven to cool. Not to mention the whole resting it overnight in the fridge thing. If you're impatient like I am, then this is a massive test of will. But I promise that all these steps mean you will be rewarded with a thick, creamy cheesecake that tastes delicious. It may be a slow process but it's perfect if you want to get dessert done and out of the way, so you can take slices from it as and when. The warmth of the nutmeg in this cheesecake works especially well when paired with the sharpness of the orange.

For the base

250g digestive biscuits

115g unsalted butter, melted

For the filling

500g full-fat cream cheese

200g caster sugar

4 medium eggs

300ml whipping cream

2 tablespoons plain flour

1 teaspoon ground nutmeg

1 tablespoon lemon juice

2 teaspoons vanilla extract

To serve

200ml whipping cream, whipped

2 large oranges, peeled and segmented

ground nutmeg, for sprinkling

Prep: 30 minutes, plus chilling and cooling
Cook: 1 hour   ❄: Can be frozen without topping

To make the base: Lightly grease a 23cm round loose-bottomed tin.

Blitz the biscuits in a food processer until they resemble fine breadcrumbs. Add the melted butter and process again for a few seconds to mix.

Press the crumbs into the base of the tin, then chill for 1 hour in the fridge.

To make the filling: Preheat the oven to 180°C/fan 160°C.

Beat the cream cheese and sugar together with a handheld mixer for a minute, then add the eggs and cream. Mix for about 3 minutes on medium.

Now add the flour, nutmeg, lemon juice and vanilla extract, and continue mixing to combine. Pour the mixture on to the chilled crust.

Bake in the oven for 1 hour, or until the cheesecake is golden brown on the edges – it should still have a very slight wobble in the middle if you shake it gently. Turn off the oven and let the cheesecake sit in the oven for 2 hours. Then open the oven door and let it stand for another hour. Letting it cool slowly like this will help prevent the cheesecake from cracking.

Put the cheesecake in the fridge to chill overnight.

To serve: Take the cheesecake out of the tin.

Top with the whipped cream, then arrange the orange segments on top and sprinkle with nutmeg.

Her Majesty's cake

For the cake

700g plain flour, sifted

4 teaspoons baking powder

500g unsalted softened butter, diced

500g caster sugar

8 medium eggs

3 tablespoons lemon juice

zest of 3 oranges

For the buttercream

400g unsalted butter, softened

800g icing sugar, sifted

zest of 2 oranges

4 tablespoons whole milk

For the fondant drizzle

150g white fondant, grated

25ml water

purple food colouring

For the orange drizzle

juice of 3 oranges (you need about 200–300ml)

150g caster sugar

For decoration

white sugarpaste roses, varying sizes, or real roses

edible glue or glucose syrup

edible silver glitter

I didn't ever think I was going to say these words all in one sentence: 'I made the Queen's 90th birthday cake!' Being asked to do this was probably one of my proudest moments. However, when the realization struck, I was rather flummoxed. I mean, what kind of cake could I possibly make that the Queen would enjoy; what design, size, flavour, colour, type of cake should it be? After deliberating for days, I decided to opt for a classic drizzle cake, but flavoured with oranges rather than lemons, with a vibrant purple fondant and decorated with roses. I knew that my cake was never going to be as opulent or have as much grandeur as some of the Queen's past birthday cakes, but I'm incredibly proud of it. Here is a smaller, simpler version for you to try at home – you can choose whether to go for a simple drizzle cake, or to decorate it with the fondant and the roses.

Prep: **50 minutes to 1 hour**   Cook: **1¼ to 1¾ hours**
❄: **Sponges can be frozen before decorating and drizzling**

For the cake, line and grease 2 x 20cm springform tins. Preheat the oven to 180°C/fan 160°C. Add all the ingredients to a bowl one by one then, using a handheld or stand mixer, mix everything together for 3 minutes till you have a smooth batter. Divide the mixture between two tins and level off the tops. Bake for 1½ hours to 1¾ hours, but check it after 1¼ hours as it will depend on your oven. While the cakes are cooking you can get on and make the buttercream and drizzles.

To make the buttercream, add the butter to a mixing bowl and mix on high for 2 minutes. Add the icing sugar a little at a time and mix on a medium speed. Add the milk and orange zest and mix on a high speed for 3 minutes until you have a light and fluffy buttercream.

When the cakes are golden brown, with a slight peak at the top, and a skewer inserted comes out clean, they are ready. Remove from the oven and leave to cool for 10 minutes in the tin. Turn out and leave to cool completely on a wire rack. Cut the domed tops off both sponges and level them off. Carefully slice both cakes across into two, giving you four sponges.

To make the orange drizzle, add the orange juice and sugar to a jug and mix well. The sugar will not dissolve completely. Spoon the mixture equally over the 4 sponges.

Lay the four sponges out, making sure that one of the two with crusts faces down and one faces up. Then generously cover the top and side of each with the buttercream. Put the crust-side-down slice on a cake base or plate then carefully place the other layers on top, finishing with the crust-side-up slice. Place the whole cake in the fridge or in a cool place for about 15-20 minutes until the buttercream has crusted over.

Now make the fondant drizzle. Add the grated fondant and water to a pan and heat on low to medium, stirring constantly, until it has melted and become a liquid. Add the food colouring a little at a time until you have a vibrant purple colour. Transfer into a bowl and leave to cool completely. Add a drop or two of cold water to loosen, if needed.

Pour the cold purple fondant over the top of the cake, drizzling it gently down the sides. Then finish off the decoration by brushing the tips of the sugar paste roses with edible glue and dipping them in glitter. Arrange them in a crescent shape around one edge of the top of the cake. Or simply decorate it using real white roses.

Parsnip and orange spiced cake

Serves 10

Now, before you say it – yes, there are parsnips in this cake. My parents love a good carrot cake, but when it's the only thing they ask me to bake because they are not adventurous enough for much else . . . well, I had to change it up just for my own creative sanity. Carrots may give colour, but parsnips add a similar flavour and sweetness with a whole lot more fragrance, so this isn't as bold and daring as it might sound from the title. It's a moist and delicious cake, and an excellent alternative to carrot. You could also give this recipe a go with courgette or beetroot. They all add different things and work equally well.

For the sponge

230g self-raising flour

1 teaspoon baking powder

1 teaspoon ground cinnamon

½ teaspoon ground nutmeg

2 teaspoons ground mixed spice

200g caster sugar

100g walnuts, chopped, plus extra for topping

3 medium eggs

150ml sunflower oil

500g parsnips, peeled, ends trimmed and coarsely grated

zest of 2 oranges, plus extra for decoration

For the frosting

50g unsalted butter, softened

200g full-fat cream cheese

150g icing sugar

zest of 1 orange

Prep: 25 minutes   Cook: 30 minutes   ❄: Sponges can be frozen

To make the cake: Preheat the oven to 180°C/fan 160°C. Grease and line the base of two 20.5cm sandwich tins with baking paper.

In a large bowl sift together the flour, baking powder, cinnamon, nutmeg and mixed spice. Add the caster sugar and chopped walnuts, mix through with a wooden spoon, and set aside.

Put the eggs and sunflower oil in a different bowl, and beat for a few minutes. Now mix all the dry ingredients into the egg and oil mixture, along with the the grated parsnips and orange zest. Mix everything together until you have a thick batter; about 2 minutes.

Divide the mixture between the two cake tins, and level it off using a spatula. Bake for 25–30 minutes. The cakes should be golden, and a skewer inserted into the centre should come out clean.

Leave the cakes in the tins for 10 minutes, then turn out on to a wire rack and peel off the baking paper. Leave to cool completely.

To make the frosting: In a bowl, beat the butter with a wooden spoon then add the cream cheese and icing sugar. Beat until it all comes together, but be careful not to overdo it, or the frosting will become runny. Leave the frosting in the fridge until you need it, if your kitchen is really warm.

Take your cooled cakes and sandwich them together using the frosting. Top the cake with lashings of frosting and sprinkle with walnuts, and some extra orange zest.

Raspberry jam puddle brownies

Makes 18

Many years ago, my husband absolutely detested brownies. We bought them once, he referred to them as 'uncooked cold cake', and we never returned to them until I decided to bake a batch soon after my first son was born. I presented the finished brownies to my husband with bated breath – I always want him to love everything I bake. He doesn't always, but I needed to change his mind about brownies. All I can say is, we have never looked back. He has adored them ever since, and we have tried so many variations. This is a standard brownie with a crisp top, but with the addition of pools of raspberry jam dotted around to make for gooey chocolate gorgeousness with surprising bursts of tangy fruit.

275g unsalted butter, softened

375g caster sugar

4 medium eggs

75g cocoa powder

100g self-raising flour

100g dark chocolate chips

100g seedless raspberry jam

Prep: **20 minutes**   Cook: **45–50 minutes**   ❄: **Can be frozen**

Preheat the oven to 180°C/fan 160°C. Grease and line a 30 x 23 x 4cm baking tin.

Put the butter, sugar, eggs, cocoa powder and self-raising flour in a stand mixer, and mix on medium for 2 minutes. This will take around 5 minutes with a handheld mixer.

Now add the chocolate chips and mix them through using a spatula.

Pour the mixture into the tin and spread it out evenly using a spatula, making sure to poke it into all the corners.

Now dot teaspoons of jam all over the brownie mixture, making sure there are gaps between the puddles.

Bake for 40–45 minutes, until the brownie has a slight crust on top.

Leave the brownie to cool in the tin before cutting it into squares to serve.

Sour cherry and almond Bundt cake

Serves 10

I love making a good hearty Bundt cake, mainly because it needs very little doing to it. All the flavour is in the cake, with the sour cherries and the almond extract in the batter. All it wants is a dusting of icing sugar to finish it off. It's great with a scoop of ice cream or hot custard, or just on its own with a cup of tea.

125g unsalted butter, softened

170g caster sugar

2 medium eggs

100g ground almonds

125g self-raising flour

185g plain flour, plus extra for dusting

1 heaped teaspoon baking powder

125ml whole milk

1 teaspoon almond extract

680g Morello cherries, pitted and drained, or you can use tinned as long as they're drained and towel dried

Prep: 25 minutes   **Cook: 50 minutes**   ❄: **Can be frozen**

Preheat the oven to 180°C/fan 160°C. Lightly grease a 23cm Bundt or rum baba tin. Flour the inside of the greased tin, tapping out the excess.

Cream the butter and sugar until fluffy using a stand or handheld mixer if you have one.

Add the eggs one by one, beating well after each addition. Stir in the ground almonds.

Now mix in the flour, the baking powder and the milk along with the almond extract, alternating between spoonfuls of flour and liquid. Finally, add the cherries and fold them through with a spatula.

Spoon the batter into the tin, and level off with a spatula.

Bake for 50 minutes, or until a skewer inserted into the centre comes out clean and the top is golden.

Leave the cake to cool in the tin for 10 minutes, then turn out on to a wire rack. When it is completely cool, dust with icing sugar.

Strawberry and mint Swiss roll

Serves 6

When I entered the realm of competitive baking it was tough for a person like me – I am competitive with myself, but nobody else. So with no choice but to 'bake fight' I had to pull out all the stops. It forced me to stop thinking within the confines and comfort of my own box and venture out of my square world. This is when I discovered how well herbs and fruit go together. The strawberry and mint in this jam work so well together; once cooled, it tastes just like fruit pastille sweets. It took me right back to childhood, and now I have to have this jam mixture in my Swiss roll. For me, there's nothing more nostalgic.

For the jam

200g strawberries,
  hulled and chopped

200g jam sugar

a large handful of fresh
  mint, chopped

For the sponge

3 medium eggs

75g caster sugar

75g plain flour

a pinch of fine sea salt

50g caster sugar, half
  for dusting the baking
  paper and half for
  sprinkling over at
  the end

For the filling

150ml whipping cream

½ teaspoon vanilla
  bean paste

Prep: **20 minutes**   Cook: **20 minutes**   ❄: **Cannot be frozen**

To make the jam: Put the strawberries and the jam sugar in a heavy bottomed pan over a high heat, and heat until the jam mixture reaches 105°C.

As soon as it reaches the right temperature, take it off the heat, strain it through a sieve and leave it to cool.

Once it is cool enough to touch, add the chopped mint, and stir to combine. Now, I urge you to taste it. Please tell me you can taste fruit pastilles!

Leave the jam to chill in the fridge.

To make the sponge: Preheat the oven to 220°C/fan 200°C. Grease a 20 x 30cm Swiss roll tin, and line it with baking paper.

Put the eggs in a stand mixer or whisk with a handheld mixer until they are frothy. Add the caster sugar and continue to whisk until the mixture is frothy and light and has doubled in volume. The mixture should be thick and pale. Draw a figure of eight in the mixture using a whisk – if it remains for more than 3 seconds the mixture has reached the ribbon stage, and is ready.

Sift the flour and salt into the whisked egg and sugar mixture. Fold in using a large metal spoon, very gently and making sure that you don't remove all the air.

Pour the mixture into the tin, making sure it gets into all the corners. Bake for 8–10 minutes. The sides should just come away from the tin, and the sponge should be golden and springy.

Sprinkle a large sheet of baking paper with half of the caster sugar, and tip out the sponge on top. Peel off the baking paper from the sponge.

Use a sharp knife to make a shallow cut about 2cm in from one of the short ends of the sponge. This will neaten it and expose the swirls.

Now, roll up the sponge starting from the cut end, making sure to take the paper underneath with you so the paper is rolled inside.

Put the roll on a wire rack, and leave it to cool.

To make the filling: Whip up the cream with the vanilla bean paste, to soft peaks.

Unroll the sponge and smother it on one side with copious amounts of the jam, leaving a 2cm border around the edge.

Cover the jam with the whipped cream, again leaving a 2cm gap around all the edges.

Now roll the whole thing up again, starting from the cut short edge, taking the paper away as you roll.

Sprinkle the finished Swiss roll with the remaining caster sugar.

Dinner date

Married at twenty, and with an enormous move to Yorkshire, I then had my first little man at twenty-one and have since had two more beautiful kids. It's safe to say that life moved fast. I've found that being a stay-at-home mum can be the most laborious yet satisfying job ever, but with my husband working long hours, finding alone time was near-enough impossible. So we decided a few years ago that we had to actively set some time aside for ourselves, even if it was as little as once a month. It might not seem much, but it was more than we had before. Date nights for us have been a saving grace, and we take it in turns: one month it is up to me to decide what we do, the next it is Abdal's turn. I naturally lean towards cooking a meal – something quick, easy and special, so I can spend less time in the kitchen and more time with my best friend. These evenings are so special to us; I always cook his favourites, and these are a few of them.

Beef steak and pepper noodle stir-fry • Almond floating islands

This aromatic stir-fry is quick and easy to make. It's also wholesome – with the slices of steak – and fresh, with the added crunch of the quickly cooked vegetables. The dessert, with its light vanilla custard and fluffy almond meringues, works really well to follow.

Beef steak and pepper noodle stir-fry

_____

Serves 2

For the marinade

250g beef steak, thinly sliced into strips

1 teaspoon mirin (rice wine)

¼ teaspoon fine sea salt

1½ teaspoons dark soy sauce

1½ teaspoons cornflour

For the stir-fry

2 tablespoons vegetable oil

2.5cm piece of ginger, peeled and finely chopped

2 cloves of garlic, finely chopped

1 red chilli, deseeded and chopped (seeds in if you like it hotter)

½ red pepper

½ yellow pepper

1 teaspoon Chinese five-spice

1 teaspoon chilli flakes

3 spring onions, green parts finely chopped on the diagonal

1 small pack, (100g) of noodles, soaked in boiling water

1 teaspoon sesame oil

Prep: **15 minutes**   Cook: **10 minutes**   ❄: **Cannot be frozen**

To marinate the beef: Put the beef strips in a bowl. Add the mirin, salt, soy sauce and cornflour.

Give everything a really good mix with your hands and set the beef aside while you prepare all the vegetables. It is essential that these are all ready to go, because once that wok is heated everything goes into it very quickly.

To make the stir-fry: Put a large wok over a very high heat, until it starts smoking. Now add the oil. Next add the marinated beef, making sure each strip is cooked, but don't overcook them.

Put the cooked beef in a clean bowl, and set aside.

Now, using the oil still in the wok, add the ginger, garlic and chilli. Cook for 10 seconds, making sure not to burn it.

Now add the red and yellow pepper, Chinese five-spice, chilli flakes and spring onions. Cook over a high heat for 2 minutes, stirring constantly.

Add the beef and cook for another 2 minutes.

Now drain the noodles, add to the mix and stir. Take the wok off the heat, add the sesame oil, and mix it once more.

Almond floating islands

Serves 2

For the meringue:

2 egg whites

60g caster sugar

1 teaspoon almond extract

For the vanilla custard

200ml single cream

100ml whole milk, plus a little extra

1 vanilla pod

3 whole eggs

2 egg yolks

60g caster sugar

For the topping

20g slivered almonds, toasted

Prep: 25 minutes, plus cooking   Cook: **10 minutes**
❄: **Cannot be frozen**

To make the meringues: Whisk the egg whites until they form soft peaks. Gradually add the caster sugar, a spoonful at a time, until the sugar is all incorporated. Keep whisking all the time, until the mixture is fluffy and glossy.

Finally, add the almond extract and mix well.

To make the vanilla custard: Put the cream and milk in a wide shallow pan with the vanilla pod and bring to a simmer over a low heat.

Float generous dessertspoonfuls of the meringue mixture on the top of the cream and milk. Be careful not to overcrowd the pan. Cook the meringues for 1 minute on each side.

Remove them with a slotted spoon and place them on a plate.

Strain the hot cream and milk mixture through a sieve into a jug. Top up with extra milk to get it to 300ml.

Pour the mixture into a saucepan with the split vanilla pod, and scrape out the seeds. Bring the mixture to the boil, then take it off the heat.

Whisk the eggs, egg yolks and sugar together in a large bowl.

Slowly add the hot milk and cream mixture to the egg mixture, making sure to keep stirring all the time. Put everything back into the pan and keep stirring with a wooden spoon over a low heat, until the custard coats the back of the spoon. If the custard curdles, give it a quick whizz with a handheld blender to bring it back.

Pour the custard into a shallow serving dish and place the meringues on top. Top with the toasted almond slivers.

Fresh sea bass fennel ceviche • Chocolate coffee terrine

This is one of my favourite dinner-date combinations. In fact, it works for any occasion where you want to prepare things beforehand. The purpose of our dinner dates is to spend quality time with one another, and these recipes allow for exactly that. The ceviche is light, fresh and zingy – not filling, but made more satisfying with some crusty bread. It can be made hours in advance. And the terrine can be made the day before, so that's that done too. The deep flavour of the coffee and chocolate give a grown-up taste . . . with not a coloured sprinkle in sight.

Fresh sea bass fennel ceviche

Serves 2

250g very fresh sea bass fillets, skinned

350g cherry tomatoes, quartered

½ medium red onion, thinly sliced

50g fennel, thinly sliced

1 garlic clove, crushed

3 tablespoons olive oil, plus extra for drizzling

1 tablespoon cider vinegar

a large handful of fresh mint, coarsely torn

salt and freshly ground black pepper, to taste

crusty bread, to serve

Prep: 15 minutes plus 3 hours marinating   ❄: Cannot be frozen

Cut the fillets of fish at an angle, in slices about ½cm thick, and put them in a large bowl.

Add the tomatoes, red onion, fennel, garlic, olive oil, cider vinegar and mint, and season with salt and pepper. Use your hands to mix everything together, taking care not to break up the fish.

Cover the bowl and leave it in the fridge for at least 3 hours, making sure to turn the mixture a few times. This will help to ensure that all the acids coat the fish, effectively 'cooking' it.

Take the ceviche out of the fridge 1 hour before serving to bring it to room temperature.

Serve drizzled with olive oil, and with plenty of crusty bread on the side.

Chocolate coffee terrine

Serves 2

115g unsalted butter, plus extra for greasing

65g dark chocolate (70% cocoa solids)

4 medium egg yolks

65g caster sugar

40g cocoa powder

a pinch of fine sea salt

170ml double cream

5g espresso powder

20g icing sugar

crème fraîche, quartered strawberries and chocolate-covered coffee beans, to serve

Prep: 20 minutes plus overnight for chilling ❄: Cannot be frozen

Line the inside of two ramekins with clingfilm. The best way is to grease the inside of the ramekin with butter, and then line it. Chop the chocolate and butter into chunks, then put them in a bowl, and melt in the microwave or in a heatproof bowl over a simmering pan of water. Be careful not to overheat and burn the chocolate.

Put the egg yolks and sugar in another bowl, and whisk with a handheld mixer for about 5 minutes, until the mixture is fluffy.

Now sift the cocoa powder and salt into the egg mixture, and keep mixing. The mixture should become stiff. Set it aside.

Put the cream, espresso powder and icing sugar in a small pan and bring it to the boil, then take it off the heat.

Add the melted chocolate and butter mixture to the egg mixture, whisking all the time. You should have a thick paste.

Pour the hot cream, just off the boil, slowly into the chocolate paste mixture, stirring all the time.

When it is all incorporated, pass it through a sieve to remove any lumps, then pour into the prepared ramekins, and put it in the fridge overnight.

To serve, place the ramekins into a roasting dish filled with hot water. This should release the edges of the terrines.

Turn the terrines upside down on to a plate. Remove the ramekins and clingfilm, then serve with crème fraîche, quartered strawberries and chocolate-covered coffee beans.

Crusted rack of lamb with aubergine bortha • Strawberry curd tartlets

These two recipes are my attempts at being a little bit fancier. The herby rack of lamb partnered with the zesty aubergines tastes as vibrant as it looks. I like to cook the rack rare, but you can cook it to your liking. It doesn't need sauce, as the aubergines are moist and flavourful. The meal is finished off with crisp tartlets filled with buttery, strawberry-scented curd. This recipe makes 24 little tartlets, so there will be plenty left over.

Crusted rack of lamb with aubergine bortha

Serves 2

For the aubergine bortha

1 large aubergine

2 tablespoons olive oil

2 cloves of garlic, crushed

1 small red onion, finely chopped

½ teaspoon fine sea salt

1 teaspoon cumin seeds

a handful of fresh coriander, chopped

a handful of fresh mint, chopped

zest of ½ lemon

For the crusted lamb

2 tablespoons vegetable oil, for frying

1 rack of lamb, with 6 bones

2 thick slices of stale bread, white or wholemeal

a small bunch each of fresh parsley and mint

2 tablespoons English mustard, plus extra for brushing

a pinch of salt and freshly ground black pepper

Prep: 20 minutes   Cook: 30–45 minutes, plus 10 minutes resting time
❄: **Cannot be frozen**

To make the aubergine bortha: Pierce the aubergine all over and cover it in clingfilm. Microwave it on full power for 8–10 minutes; it will become deflated and wilted-looking. Alternatively, you could pierce the aubergine and bake it at 200°C/fan 180°C for 30 minutes. Leave to cool, so it's easier to handle, then cut it in half and scoop out all the flesh. Use a fork to mash up the flesh.

Put the olive oil in a medium non-stick pan over a medium heat. Add the garlic, red onion, salt and cumin seeds, and cook, stirring occasionally, for 3 minutes. Now add the aubergine, and cook for a further 6–8 minutes, until the aubergine is quite dry.

Take off the heat, and add the coriander, mint and lemon zest. Stir to combine.

To make the crusted lamb: Preheat the oven to 200°C/fan 180°C. Heat the oil in a large non-stick pan over a high heat. Sprinkle the rack of lamb with salt and pepper, and brown on all sides, making sure to cook off as much fat as you can. This should take about 5 minutes. Set the rack aside to cool.

Put the bread, parsley, mint and English mustard in the food processor, and whizz until you have a mixture with the texture of breadcrumbs. Brush the top of the rack with more mustard, and pat the breadcrumb mixture on to it.

Place the rack on a roasting dish and bake in an oven at 200. Cook for 12–15 minutes, or to your liking.

Strawberry curd tartlets

Serves 24

For the pastry

150g plain flour, plus extra for rolling

100g cold unsalted butter, cut into small cubes

2 tablespoons icing sugar

1 medium egg yolk

For the strawberry curd

150g strawberries, hulled

100g unsalted butter, melted

100g caster sugar

3 medium eggs, beaten

24 dehydrated strawberries, chopped

24 small sprigs of mint

icing sugar, for dusting

Prep: 30 minutes   Cook: **12 minutes, plus 2 hours chilling time**

❋: **Cannot be frozen**

To make the pastry: Preheat the oven to 180°C/fan 160°C.

Put the flour in a bowl, then add the butter to the flour and rub in until it resembles breadcrumbs. Alternatively, you can use a food processor. Add the icing sugar and mix the dough thoroughly by hand. Add the egg yolk, then use a palette knife to mix it in.

Using your hands, bring the dough together into a ball. If it doesn't come together easily, add tablespoonfuls of water until it does.

Wrap the pastry in clingfilm, flatten and chill for 30 minutes in the fridge.

Put the pastry on a floured surface and roll out to about 2mm thick. Use a suitably sized round cutter to cut out circles to line a 24-hole mini muffin tray.

Put small pieces of greaseproof paper inside each pastry case and fill with baking beans. Bake for 12 minutes, then take the cases out of the oven, take out the paper and beans and bake for another 5 minutes.

Gently take the pastry shells out of the muffin tin and leave them on a wire rack to cool.

To make the strawberry curd: Whizz the strawberries in a food processor until you have a liquid. Pass them through a sieve to remove any seeds or lumps, and set aside.

Put the melted butter, sugar and eggs in a bowl over a pan of simmering water, and gently stir the curd with a wooden spoon, until it thickens and will coat the back of the spoon.

Take the curd off the heat and add the strawberry liquid. Transfer it to another bowl and chill it in the fridge for 2 hours.

Once the curd has cooled, put it into a piping bag and pipe it into the tart shells. Top each tart with a sprinkle of dehydrated strawberry pieces and a sprig of mint, and dust with a little icing sugar.

Gnocchi with cheese, pine nuts and rocket • Lychee, lemon and passionfruit jelly

Although I love my husband, one thing we don't always have in common is our taste in food. So often when I cook for us, we have a little bit of something he likes and a little bit of something I like. After all, compromise is key (as long as he understands that I am always right). He is not a massive fan of cheese, while I could live on the stuff. He loves jelly like a big kid, but gelatine and juice really aren't my thing. So this is our compromise meal. We have warm gnocchi with cheese, pine nuts and a hint of nutmeg, and fresh rocket. Then a light, fragrant, fruity jelly with the crunch of passionfruit seeds.

Gnocchi with cheese, pine nuts and rocket

Serves 4, or 2 with leftovers

For the gnocchi

750g floury mashed potato, prepared without butter or milk and left to cool completely

1 medium egg yolk, beaten

125g plain flour, plus extra for dusting

1 tablespoon olive oil, for frying

salt and freshly ground black pepper, to taste, plus 1 teaspoon fine sea salt

For the cheese sauce

100ml single cream

50g Stilton, finely grated

½ teaspoon freshly grated nutmeg

50g mature Cheddar cheese, finely grated

50g toasted pine nuts

rocket, to serve

Prep: 15–20 minutes (if you have the mash prepared and cooled)
Cook: 10 minutes ❄: Can be frozen

Have some mash prepared but with nothing like butter or milk added. Leave it to cool completely. To this add the egg yolk, flour and salt and pepper to taste. Mix everything together well to form a soft dough.

Put the dough on a lightly floured surface. Divide the dough into four pieces. Knead each piece lightly and roll it into a long sausage about 2cm in diameter, then cut it into 3cm sections. Roll these into balls and press the tops with a fork to make indentations. Place the gnocchi on a floured tray, and set aside. These can be left in the fridge for 24 hours, or frozen for 1 month, but for this recipe place in the fridge for half an hour just to chill and firm up the gnocchi.

To make the cheese sauce put the cream and stilton in a small pan over a medium heat until the cheese has melted. Grate in some nutmeg, and set the sauce aside.

Now put a large saucepan of water on the hob to boil. Add 1 teaspoon of salt to the water. Reduce the heat until the water is at a gentle rolling boil, then add the gnocchi in batches, making sure not to overcrowd the pan.

The gnocchi will take 1–2 minutes to cook. You will know they are ready when they rise to the top. Use a slotted spoon to pick up the gnocchi and drain them in a colander.

Once all the gnocchi are cooked and drained, fry them lightly in a non-stick pan, with the olive oil. This will help to crisp the edges slightly before baking. You may need to do this in batches; once fried, set aside.

Place the gnocchi in a heatproof dish and pour over the cheese sauce, then gently mix everything together.

Sprinkle over the pine nuts, then the grated Cheddar and put the dish under a hot grill for 2 minutes.

Top with the rocket and a grinding of black pepper to serve.

Lychee, lemon and passionfruit jelly

Serves 4, or 2 with leftovers

7 gelatine leaves, or 3 tablespoons of gelatine powder

475ml lychee juice

juice of 1 small lemon

60g castor sugar

3 passionfruit, insides scooped out

Prep: **10 minutes**   Cook: **5 minutes**   ❄: **Can be frozen**

If you are using gelatine leaves, soak them in cold water and set aside. If you are using powdered gelatine, add it to 6 tablespoons of water.

Put the lychee juice, lemon juice and sugar in a pan over a medium heat, until the sugar has dissolved. Take the pan off the heat and set it aside to cool significantly.

Once the juice and sugar mixture has cooled, microwave the gelatine (if you are using powdered gelatine) for 10-second bursts. Once it has dissolved, add it to the mixture.

If you are using gelatine leaves, squeeze out any excess water and add the leaves to the warm juice, then leave the juice to cool to room temperature.

Pour the jelly into moulds to set, and leave it in the fridge for 30 minutes.

Add the passionfruit to the partially set jelly, and give it a good mix through. This will mean that the seeds are suspended in the jelly

Put the jelly back in the fridge and allow it to set for 2–3 hours before serving.

Crispy filo with seared tuna • Quick chocolate, banana and peanut butter ice cream

I love tuna, even in its canned incarnation, but fresh tuna is always a bit of a treat – I love to cook it rare. This wasn't my husband's favourite way of eating it, but I soon changed his mind. You can always cook it for longer if you prefer it well done. The crisp shells filled with salad and warm tuna are beautifully light and leave enough room for something sweet. I like to use readymade filo, but if you have the time and patience to make it yourself, go for it! Meanwhile, dessert is a fast banana ice cream recipe that is best made together in the kitchen when it's time for afters. The frozen ripe bananas are the magic ingredient; everything else can be adapted and changed to suit your taste.

Crispy filo with seared tuna

Serves 2

For the crispy filo

10 x 10cm square pieces of filo pastry

1 tablespoon olive oil

For the seared tuna

160g fresh tuna steaks

1 tablespoon cracked black peppercorns

fine sea salt, to taste

2 tablespoons olive oil

15g unsalted butter

For the salad

1 tablespoon balsamic vinegar

2 tablespoons olive oil

80g rocket leaves

8 cherry tomatoes, quartered

8 black olives, pitted and sliced

2 hardboiled eggs, quartered

Prep: **20 minutes**   Cook: **15 minutes**   ❄: **Cannot be frozen**

To make the crispy filo: Preheat the oven to 170°C/fan 150°C. Brush the inside of two 10cm loose-bottomed tart tins with olive oil.

Put five pieces of filo pastry into each tart tin. As you put each square in, brush it with olive oil. When layering, make sure the corners don't match up, so you end up with a star with lots of points.

Put the filo cases in their tins on a baking sheet, and place a small piece of baking paper inside each and fill it with baking beans.

Bake for 10 minutes. Remove the baking beans and paper. Bake for a further three minutes to ensure they're cooked and golden, then remove the crispy shells and leave them to cool on a wire rack, ready for when you need them. (You can make them in advance and store in an airtight container.)

To make the seared tuna: Put the tuna steaks on a plate, and sprinkle with the cracked black pepper and salt.

Put the oil and butter in a non-stick pan over a high heat. When the butter has melted add the tuna and cook for 1 minute on each side if you like it rare, 2 minutes on each side if you like it medium or 3 minutes on each side if you like it well done. Set the cooked tuna aside.

To make the salad: Mix the balsamic vinegar and the oil together in a small bowl to make a simple dressing.

Put the rocket leaves, tomatoes and olives into a larger serving bowl. Mix the dressing through the salad.

Divide the salad between the two filo cases, then arrange the egg quarters on top.

Slice the tuna and place it on top of the salad.

Quick chocolate, banana and peanut butter ice cream

Serves 2

2 large ripe bananas, sliced into coins and frozen for at least 2 hours

1 tablespoon crunchy peanut butter

1 tablespoon cocoa powder

a pinch of fine sea salt

2 tablespoons salted peanuts, roughly chopped

Prep: 10 minutes, plus two hours freezing

Put the frozen banana into a small food processor, and whizz. You may need to let the slices defrost for a few minutes first, so that they soften slightly. It will start to break up. Stop the machine at intervals and scrape the banana down the sides. Keep blitzing until it forms a paste.

Now add the peanut butter, cocoa and a pinch of salt. Mix again.

Sprinkle with the chopped salted peanuts to serve.

Meatloaf and hasselback potatoes •
Iced summer fruits with lemon white chocolate sauce

This recipe is kind of a balancing act. The meatloaf requires time in the kitchen, preparing the different stages – from cooking the meatloaf, to timing it with the potatoes and making the gravy. It's a hearty dish, with a rich sauce, and my alternative to chips is the hasselback potatoes. All of which is why I have kept the dessert that follows as simple and easy as possible. The frozen berries need little embellishment, and the sauce takes mere minutes to make. But the combination of hot and cold, and of tart berries with sweet lemon infused chocolate creaminess, is a match made in heaven.

Meatloaf and hasselback potatoes

Serves 2

Prep: **30 minutes**   Cook: **1 hour**   ❄: **Cannot be frozen**

For the meatloaf

40g semolina

50ml hot beef stock

250g beef mince

½ small onion, grated

1 egg yolk

1 teaspoon mustard

½ teaspoon freshly ground black pepper

½ teaspoon fine sea salt

6–8 turkey rashers

For the sauce

1 tablespoon salted butter

1 tablespoon plain flour

hot water

salt and freshly ground black pepper, to taste

1 tablespoon tomato ketchup

1 tablespoon single cream

To make the meatloaf: Preheat the oven to 200°C/fan 180°C.

Put the semolina and hot stock in a bowl, and leave the grains to absorb the liquid.

Put the mince, onion, egg yolk, mustard in another bowl, and season with salt and pepper. Mix it all together by hand, then add the semolina and stock mixture and mix again.

Put the meat mixture into the ovenproof dish and form it into a loaf shape. Cover the meatloaf with the turkey rashers, making sure to tuck them in underneath.

Bake in the oven for 20 minutes. Take it out of the oven, turn the temperature down to 175°C/fan 155°C and pour 120ml water into the bottom of the dish, then cook for a further 20 minutes.

To make the hasselback potatoes: Cut slices all across the potatoes and two-thirds of the way down, making sure not to cut right through. The slices should be 3mm apart.

Put the potatoes into an ovenproof dish and drizzle with oil, then put into the oven at the same time as the meatloaf, then bake for 20 minutes.

Melt the butter in the microwave or a small pan on the hob, just before you take out the potatoes. Drizzle the potatoes with the butter, making sure to get it into the cuts, then bake for another

4 medium roasting
  potatoes

oil, for drizzling

3 tablespoons salted
  butter

25g breadcrumbs

20 minutes. You will know they are done when potatoes don't resist when squashed with fingers. If the potatoes need a bit of extra time, remove the meatloaf and cover it with foil while you give the potatoes another 5 minutes.

Once the potatoes are done, sprinkle them with the breadcrumbs.

To make the sauce: Melt the butter in a small pan over a medium heat, then add the flour. Now add the liquid from the bottom of the meatloaf pan, plus a little more water if you need to.

Season with salt and pepper, then add the ketchup, and cook the sauce until it thickens. It should be quite thick. Stir through the cream.

Iced summer fruits with lemon white chocolate sauce

Serves 2   Prep: **5 minutes**   Cook: **5 minutes**   ❄: **Cannot be frozen**

250ml double cream

zest of 1 lemon

1 teaspoon Sicilian lemon
  extract

200g white chocolate
  chips

300g frozen summer fruits

Put the cream in a small pan over a medium heat until it just comes to the boil – but don't let it actually boil. Take it off the heat and add the lemon zest and extract, stirring to combine.

Now add the white chocolate chips, and leave it to sit a few moments for the chocolate to melt. After 2 minutes give it a stir, and make sure the chocolate's all melted.

Take the berries out of the freezer and spread them out on a plate in one even layer. Pour over the warm chocolate cream, and enjoy immediately.

Cosy evenings & midnight feasts

I spend all day cooking and preparing food, along with all the other things that need doing in and around my home and for my family. Every now and again we have a thing in our house where we tell the kids that we will wake them up for a midnight feast. On that day I will tinker about the house for a few hours after their bedtime, then I walk up the stairs wearily, arguing with my conscience about whether it's good parental practice to wake my sleeping kids to feed them . . . only to send them back to bed after an hour. Who knows? All I know is, it makes them happy beyond their wildest dreams. There's something about being awake while all the other kids are asleep that's irresistably exciting for under-tens! I always imagine I'll have to stir them from their sweet slumber for this feast, only to find them wide awake already, like they never went to bed hours ago. So down they tumble, and the feast begins. And sometimes our midnight feast doesn't involve the kids – instead it's time to get cosy on the sofa in the evening after the children have gone to bed. A feast for two is a feast nonetheless. This isn't about skill, technique or ability. This is about embracing the fact that sometimes we put things together and miss a few steps in between, giving us a few more precious moments with those we love and something wonderful to eat at the end. That doesn't make us lazy, it makes us human.

Best fish finger butty

Makes 2

I feel this doesn't need much of an introduction. I love food in general, but I love fish fingers with a passion, and nothing more than a warm fish finger in a bap, with salad and a good sauce. This is exactly what I want at midnight, and I have even been known to make extra fish fingers so I can sneak them cold out of the fridge the next day.

8 large fish fingers, standard size

2 large white or wholemeal baps

salted butter, for spreading

a large handful of rocket leaves

2 pickled gherkins, sliced

2 tablespoons mayonnaise

2 tablespoons capers

Prep: **10 minutes**   Cook: **15 minutes**   ❄: **Cannot be frozen**

Preheat the oven and cook the fish fingers following the instructions on the packet. I cook them for 10 minutes longer, as I like them really crunchy.

Cut the baps in half, and butter both sides.

Put the salad and some sliced gherkin on the bottom half of each bap.

Smother the other half with mayonnaise and the rest of the gherkin slices.

Put the cooked fish fingers on top of the salad and gherkins, and the top half of the bap on top to complete the butty.

Big cup banana and cinnamon cake

Makes 2 x 250ml cups

Even though my oven is almost always on, it's usually turned off by midnight – unless it's a busy week, in which case I can completely forget. When I was at school our teacher taught us how to make syrup sponges in the microwave, for those of us who didn't like to use our ovens, and recently cakes in mugs have been all the rage. I love making mine in really large cups and cooking them in the oven – the microwave alters the texture too much for my liking. I love the speed and simplicity of these . . . no need for scales, just a teaspoon, a tablespoon and a couple of cups to cook in – just make sure that they're oven-safe, or you could use ovenproof ramekins as an alternative.

1 tablespoon unsalted butter, softened

1 medium egg, lightly beaten

1 tablespoon whole milk

1 ripe banana, peeled and mashed with a fork

1 teaspoon cinnamon

3 tablespoons plain flour

3 tablespoons caster sugar

½ teaspoon baking powder

Prep: **10 minutes**   Cook: **25 minutes, but can vary depending on the size of the cups**   ❄: **Cannot be frozen**

Preheat the oven to 180°C/fan 160°C. Get a baking sheet ready to put the cups or ramekins on.

Put all the ingredients in a bowl, and mix them really well, ideally using a handheld mixer.

Spoon the mixture into the cups, so it only reaches halfway up.

Put the cups on the baking sheet, and bake for 15–20 minutes, depending on the size of your cups. The cakes should be firm, spring back when touched and come away from the sides of the cups.

Remove the cups from the oven and allow to cool for a few minutes before serving with ice cream.

Buffalo chips with celery sticks

Serves 4

I may have to take this opportunity to declare my love for fries, potato chips, wedges, curly fries . . . you name it, I love it. So it is only fitting that I can find 101 different ways to eat them. Chips are quick, easy and a great blank canvas for flavour, so if there any left over after a meal, I always find a way of embellishing them. These fries are my take on buffalo wings, with spicy Tabasco, creamy blue cheese and crunchy celery.

400g oven chips

salt and freshly ground
   black pepper, to taste

tabasco

100g blue cheese

50ml soured cream

1 stick of celery, sliced
   into thin sticks, a similar
   size to chips

Prep: **10 minutes**   Cook: **25 minutes**   ❊: **Cannot be frozen**

Preheat the oven and cook the oven chips following the packet instructions. Once cooked, season them generously with salt and pepper.

Sprinkle the chips with as much or as little Tabasco sauce as you want. I prefer half the bottle, but you might want a bit less.

Put the blue cheese and the soured cream in a small saucepan over a low heat, and allow the cheese to melt over a low heat for 3–5 minutes.

Toss the celery sticks with the chips, and drizzle over the blue cheese sauce.

Churros French toast

Serves 4

I suppose the clue is in the name. This is a sweet French toast, cooked in sugar, butter and eggs. While still warm it's then dipped in a sugar and cinnamon mix. I can guarantee a mess, but I can also promise instant sweet-tooth gratification.

2 large eggs

60ml whole milk

1 teaspoon vanilla bean paste

4 slices of white bread

30g unsalted butter

2 tablespoons vegetable oil

100g caster sugar

2 teaspoons ground cinnamon

Prep: **10 minutes**   Cook: **10 minutes (2 batches, 5 minutes each)**
❄: **Cannot be frozen**

Beat the eggs, milk and vanilla bean paste in a wide, shallow bowl, then soak the bread in this eggy mixture. Soak them all and set aside on another plate. If there is any leftover egg mixture, pour it over the bread and leave it to soak.

Heat the butter and oil in a shallow non-stick frying pan over a medium heat.

Meanwhile, mix the sugar and cinnamon in another bowl.

Fry the eggy bread for 1–2 minutes on each side, until golden around the edges. You will need to do this in two batches, or two pans.

As soon as the pieces of bread are cooked, drop them straight into the sugar and cinnamon mix, and toss to coat. Serve immediately.

Easy-peasy smores

Makes 12

We love barbecues in the summer, and our favourite thing at the end of the protein-laden meal is cosying up by the dwindling embers, toasting marshmallows and sandwiching them between chocolate digestives. But we don't have to wait until summertime barbecues to enjoy smores . . . I have found a way of enjoying these beauties at home, in the wee hours, in my pyjamas.

24 digestive biscuits

12 large marshmallows

12 thin pieces of
milk chocolate
(approximately 150g)

Prep: **10 minutes**   Cook: **5 minutes**   ❄: **Cannot be frozen**

Place the 12 marshmallows on a heatproof plate and microwave on high in 10-second bursts. You will know they are ready when you touch the surface of one and your finger breaks through the top.

Place the marshmallows in a large piping bag and cut the tip if it's disposable or use a 1cm tip if it's reusable.

Top 12 of the biscuits with a piece of chocolate before piping some marshmallow on top.

Top with the second biscuit. Squeeze together – the chocolate should start melting.

Enjoy!

Hot cookie dough and ice cream

Serves 10–12

I can enjoy cookie dough in so many forms. I ate this at a chain restaurant years ago, and thought 'for goodness' sake, I can do this' – and so I did, and here it is. Warm, soft cookie dough, served fresh from the oven with ice cream. No fuss, and absolutely delicious. I tend to make the dough beforehand and use when the urge strikes.

250g plain flour

½ teaspoon bicarbonate of soda

½ teaspoon salt

170g unsalted butter, softened

300g dark muscovado sugar

1 teaspoon vanilla bean paste

1 medium egg, plus 1 egg yolk

200g dark chocolate chips

125g white chocolate chips

clotted cream ice cream, to serve

Prep: **10 minutes**   Cook: **8 minutes**

❄: **Can be frozen; will keep in the fridge for up to 1 week**

For the dough, sift the plain flour, bicarbonate of soda and salt into a bowl.

In another bowl mix together the butter, sugar, vanilla and egg, plus extra yolk, to a smooth paste.

Now add the dry ingredients and the chocolate chips, and bring the dough together.

Preheat the oven to 190°C/fan 170°C.

Press a large handful of cookie dough into a round, flat dish with sides, such as a pie dish. Use enough dough to generously cover the base of the dish.

Bake in the oven for 8 minutes, or 12 minutes if cooking straight from the fridge. Remove the dish from the oven, being careful not to burn your hands. The dough will still be quite soft. Add a large dollop of ice cream and enjoy.

Mushroom, cheese and mustard croissants

Makes 8

For so long I only ever associated croissants with sweet things, but since I realized that they can also enter the realm of savoury, the filling ideas have been piling up. I use a croissant as I would a slice of bread, trying all the fillings I would put in a sandwich. This combination of mustard, cheese and mushrooms is super-tasty and – most importantly – easy.

4 large croissants,
   sliced in half

85ml double cream

250g mature Cheddar
   cheese, grated

2 teaspoons Dijon
   mustard

200g button mushrooms,
   sliced

freshly ground black
   pepper, to taste

a large handful of chives,
   snipped

Prep: **10 minutes**　Cook: **15 minutes**　❄: **Cannot be frozen**

Preheat the oven to 180°C/fan 160°C. Put the opened-up croissants on a baking sheet, cut side facing up.

Put the cream, grated cheese and Dijon mustard in a small pan, and warm gently for about 3–5 minutes, until the cheese has melted.

Spread the melted cheese mixture all over the top of the croissant halves. Sprinkle over the sliced mushrooms, and season with pepper.

Bake in the oven for 12 minutes, until the cheese is bubbling and crisp around the edges.

Take the croissants out of the oven, sprinkle with the snipped chives and serve.

Popcorn, peanut and white chocolate slice

Makes 10–12

Popping popcorn in a pan the old-fashioned way is so much fun. As an adult even I'm astonished when I start off with kernels and end up with popped corn. It's like magic! Popcorn is great served warm, just as it comes. But it also takes flavours so well. I love both savoury and sweet, but this combination of sweet white chocolate and peanuts is great.

For the coating

500g white chocolate

100g unsalted butter, cut into cubes so it melts faster

3 tablespoons golden syrup

¼ teaspoon fine sea salt

100g roasted salted peanuts, chopped

For the popcorn

1 tablespoon vegetable oil

4 tablespoons popping corn (approximately 85g)

To drizzle

100g dark chocolate

Prep: **15 minutes, plus cooling** Cook: **10 minutes**
❄: **Cannot be frozen; best stored in airtight container at room temperature for up to 3 days**

Place the white chocolate in a heatproof bowl, and melt it in the microwave or over a pan of barely simmering water. Now add the butter, golden syrup and salt. Give it all a good mix to melt the butter then take it off the heat, pour it into a clean bowl and leave it to cool (pouring into a new bowl rather than leaving it in the hot bowl will help the mixture cool faster). Put in the fridge to cool even faster if you need to. Warm chocolate will make the corn soggy, so it needs cooling fast. Don't worry if the mixture looks a bit separated at this stage – it will come together when you mix it into the popcorn.

Put the oil in a large saucepan, for which you have a lid, over a medium heat. Add the popping corn and stir for 1–2 minutes to coat the corn with oil. Put the lid on the pan, and give it an occasional shake.

Meanwhile, line a 20cm square baking tin.

You will start to hear popping sounds. When the popping stops, take the pan off the heat.

Put all the corn on a tray in a single layer to cool. Once it has cooled, add it to the cooled white chocolate mixture, and give it a good mix, by hand or with a wooden spoon. Finally, add the chopped peanuts.

Press the mixture into the prepared tin and leave it to set.

Melt the dark chocolate, and drizzle it over the popcorn mixture. Once everything has set, cut it into slices to serve.

Toast with a spicy fried egg

Serves 1

This has to be the easiest thing in the world to do. But it feels like such an achievement when you do it at midnight, to pacify your naughty side or just your mismanaged hunger. (I always ask myself if I'm just thirsty, but I soon scrap that idea.) This is a simply a fried egg, sunny side up, with a few spices on a piece of hot buttered toast, but that doesn't lessen the sense of accomplishment.

1½ tablespoons salted butter, for spreading and frying

1 slice of white bread, preferably from a tiger loaf

1 large egg

a pinch of chilli flakes

a pinch of fine sea salt

a pinch of cumin seeds

Prep: **5 minutes**   Cook: **5 minutes**   ❄: **Cannot be frozen**

Put a non-stick frying pan over a medium heat. Add a generous tablespoon of butter and let it melt. Wait for the butter to get really hot and almost brown.

Start toasting now. I like my toast very crunchy, but toast according to your preference.

Crack the egg into the pan and fry for 3–5 minutes, until it is crispy around the edges. Baste the egg as it fries to cook the top.

Sprinkle with chilli flakes, cumin seeds and salt to taste.

Butter the toast, and slide the egg on top. I like my yolk runny so I can break the edges off the toast and dip them in.

Toasted brioche, maple cream cheese and strawberries

Makes 8

These are all ingredients we tend to have in our cupboards and fridge, so making these is usually fun and straightforward. I don't always make them for midnight feasts – I even make them for lunch guests.

4 brioche rolls, split in half lengthways

200g full-fat cream cheese

2 tablespoons maple syrup

200g strawberries, hulled and sliced (approximately 8 strawberries)

30g unsalted pistachios, shelled and roughly chopped

Prep: 15 minutes   **Cook:** 2 minutes   ❄: Cannot be frozen

Put a frying pan over a low heat and place the halved brioche rolls on it, cut side down for a few seconds. Warm them gently until the cut side is crisp and golden, then set aside.

Mix the cream cheese with maple syrup, and spread it all over the griddled brioche.

Top with the sliced strawberries, and sprinkle with pistachios.

Turkey ham and spring onion quesadillas

Makes 8

I love this recipe because it can be made with so many store-cupboard ingredients, and any you don't have are easily replaced: tuna instead of turkey ham; onions instead of spring onions; pickles instead of jalapeños; mint instead of coriander. I have even used the kids' stringy cheese if I have run out of the grown-up stuff. A quesadilla is a great wrapper for any fillings you like. Just use your imagination – you might be surprised what you come up with!

8 large flour tortillas

250g Cheddar cheese, grated

300g turkey ham, thinly sliced

8 spring onions, thinly sliced on the diagonal

6 small fresh jalapeños, thinly sliced or 115g dried jalapeños, roughly chopped

a handful of coriander leaves (1 small pack)

Prep: **5 minutes**   Cook: **5 minutes per batch** (cooked in 4 batches)   ❄: **Cannot be frozen**

Put a griddle pan on the hob, and heat until it is really hot. Once it's very hot, turn the heat down to the lowest setting.

Now assemble all your quesadillas before you start cooking. Spread out the tortillas, and sprinkle half of the cheese on to one half of each of them.

Now add the sliced turkey ham on top of the cheese, on all the tortillas. Sprinkle over the spring onion slices, and the jalapeños.

Top with the coriander leaves and the remaining grated cheese.

Fold the empty half of each tortilla over on to the half with the fillings.

Pick up the filled tortilla carefully, using a spatula or fish slice, and place it on the hot griddle pan. Use the back of the spatula to press it down flat as much as possible.

You will know when to turn the quesadilla because the two sides will be welded together with melted cheese – this will take around 3 minutes. Cooking the other side will take 1–2 minutes.

Take the quesadilla off the heat and slice it in half. Eat it while it's warm and the cheese is still stringy.

Ultimate late-night nachos

Serves 4

We always have the ingredients ready to make a massive dish of nachos: there is nothing nicer than pottering around the kitchen to put this little beauty together. As you can tell, nachos are a firm favourite in our home . . . and it seems that the more inappropriately timed and unexpected they are, the better. It's less a recipe and more just layers of flavour and texture, starting with the nachos themselves, then salsa, red onions, vinegary jalapeños and melted cheese – best eaten huddled together in front of a 1990s classic.

175g plain salted tortilla chips or pitta chips

225g jar of salsa

½ teaspoon chilli flakes

½ teaspoon ground cumin

a large handful of chopped coriander (1 small pack)

1 small red onion, thinly sliced

50g jalapeños, drained and roughly chopped

200g mature Cheddar cheese, finely grated

100ml soured cream, for dolloping

freshly ground black pepper, to taste

Prep: 10 minutes   Cook: 10 minutes   ❄: Cannot be frozen

Preheat the oven to 200°C/fan 180°C. Spread out the tortilla chips on a baking tray so there is a fairly even layer.

Tip the jar of salsa into a bowl. Add the chilli flakes, cumin and chopped coriander, then season thoroughly with pepper. Mix well, then spoon the spiced salsa all over the tortilla chips.

Spread the red onion slices evenly over the salsa and the chips, then sprinkle over the chopped jalapeños.

Finally, sprinkle over the grated cheese, and bake in the oven for 8–10 minutes. The cheese should have melted and started oozing. Parts of the nachos will be crisp.

Take the nachos out of the oven and spoon them into a serving dish, trying to retain the layers as much as possible.

Dollop teaspoons of soured cream over the hot nachos, and serve.

Cosy evenings and midnight feasts

Index

Thanks

To my best friend, my husband Abdal, for willing me to dust off the flour, for wiping my tears and propping me back up, week after week. For always seeing a sparkle that I thought faded years ago. For never following the rules so we can make new ones. Thank you for taking on the trials that we have faced over the last few months in true mummy style. You are an absolute legend!

To my three incredible children, Musa, Dawud and Maryam, who have always tried and tested everything with true enthusiasm and been pitilessly honest. For always greeting me with a daft question or a warm touch to remind me of why life is so great. Thank you for constantly reminding me of how proud you are of me, that's what makes all the hard work worth it.

To my Nan, who without realising it, taught me that it takes one extraordinary person to be the glue of the family. She is ours. She has taught me what it means to be a woman, to be independent and resilient regardless of what life throws at you. When life throws her lemons, she makes lemon chicken curry. I make lemon drizzle cake. And sometimes I make orange drizzle cake for the Queen.

To my parents, for all the trips you made to fill my freezer with meals. Thank you for being patient and understanding when times have been difficult and unfamiliar. For being the best grandparents to my children, for always babysitting on demand, without which none of this would have been possible.

To my mother- and father-in-law, for giving up so much of yourselves to allow me a future that otherwise would have been non-existent without your blessing.

To my brothers and sisters, who stepped away without complaint because I was so busy and were equally as angry because of how busy I was. Thank you for being so understanding and always reminding me that I am never too famous for a good old telling off. Thank you for always being proud and always reminding me of how loved I really am.

To my fellow *Great British Bake* off bakers, there would be no show without you guys. Thank you for giving me a once in a lifetime experience to meet eleven of the country's best bakers, who I can proudly call my friends.

To Paul and Mary, for seeing past my wavering nature and allowing me an opportunity each week. For seeing my growth and believing by the end that I was a contender. Thank you for believing in me, when I didn't believe in myself.

To Mel and Sue for giving me a shake every time I heard the words 'puff pastry'. Thank you for quiet words of support and wisdom when it felt like the world was crumbling, when actually it was just my undercooked, over-handled gingerbread. Thank you for reminding me that it will all be okay.

To Jonny, Sophie, Anna and Chloe, who saw the ugliest, saddest parts of me and sat silently and never made me feel like a fool. For looking after me, for listening to me. For making me laugh, for making me cry. For always being ready to take the most unusual pictures that best captured the experience. Long may our friendships continue.

To the Penguin team, for the support, enthusiasm and believing in my book. To Lindsey, John, Frankie, Emma, Charlotte, Holly, Sarah, Zoe and Bea. To everyone on the team who worked tirelessly to get this book together. We have learnt the hard way that recipe testing involves calories. To the gym we are bound.

To Love Productions, the BBC and the Great British Bake Off. Thank you for picking me. For giving me the first taste of self-belief. I will forever be grateful for the confidence that began to grow from the first phone call to the very last day. I can now travel on a train without the use of a brown paper bag.

To Anne, for greeting me at the end of my Bake Off journey and guiding me through the beginnings of the adventure I have always dreamed of. You are my friend, my confidante, my partner in crime. The only person who can truly appreciate printed trousers and eccentric shoes with me.